Medi Houghton, Matthew Bryant
and Veenu Jain

Cambridge IGCSE®
Enterprise

Coursebook

CAMBRIDGE
UNIVERSITY PRESS

CAMBRIDGE
UNIVERSITY PRESS

University Printing House, Cambridge CB2 8BS, United Kingdom

One Liberty Plaza, 20th Floor, New York, NY 10006, USA

477 Williamstown Road, Port Melbourne, VIC 3207, Australia

314–321, 3rd Floor, Plot 3, Splendor Forum, Jasola District Centre, New Delhi – 110025, India

103 Penang Road, #05-06/07, Visioncrest Commercial, Singapore 238467

Cambridge University Press is part of the University of Cambridge.

It furthers the University's mission by disseminating knowledge in the pursuit of education, learning and research at the highest international levels of excellence.

Information on this title: www.cambridge.org/9781108440356

© Cambridge University Press 2018

This publication is in copyright. Subject to statutory exception and to the provisions of relevant collective licensing agreements, no reproduction of any part may take place without the written permission of Cambridge University Press.

First published 2018

20 19 18 17 16 15 14 13 12 11 10 9 8 7

Printed in Poland by Opolgraf

A catalogue record for this publication is available from the British Library

ISBN 978-1-108-44035-6 Paperback
ISBN 978-1-108-33925-4 (Paperback with Cambridge Elevate Edition)
ISBN 978-1-108-44036-3 (Cambridge Elevate edition)

Additional resources for this publication at www.cambridge.org/education

Cambridge University Press has no responsibility for the persistence or accuracy of URLs for external or third-party internet websites referred to in this publication, and does not guarantee that any content on such websites is, or will remain, accurate or appropriate. Information regarding prices, travel timetables, and other factual information given in this work is correct at the time of first printing but Cambridge University Press does not guarantee the accuracy of such information thereafter.

®IGCSE is a registered trademark.

All exam-style questions and sample answers in this title were written by the authors. In examinations, the way marks are awarded may be different.

....

NOTICE TO TEACHERS IN THE UK
It is illegal to reproduce any part of this work in material form (including photocopying and electronic storage) except under the following circumstances:
(i) where you are abiding by a licence granted to your school or institution by the Copyright Licensing Agency;
(ii) where no such licence exists, or where you wish to exceed the terms of a licence, and you have gained the written permission of Cambridge University Press;
(iii) where you are allowed to reproduce without permission under the provisions of Chapter 3 of the Copyright, Designs and Patents Act 1988, which covers, for example, the reproduction of short passages within certain types of educational anthology and reproduction for the purposes of setting examination questions.

How to use this book	iv
Foreword	vii

Section 1: Identifying your enterprise project — 1

Introduction to enterprise		2
Chapter 1:	Setting up a new enterprise	11
Chapter 2:	Skills and behaviours of enterprising people	25
Chapter 3:	Opportunities, risk, legal and ethical considerations	33
	Template 1: How to conduct a PEST analysis	47
	Template 2: How to conduct a SWOT analysis	48
Chapter 4:	Market research	49
	Template 3: Conducting market research	60

Section 2: Planning your enterprise project — 62

Chapter 5:	Business planning	63
	Template 4: Action planning checklist	76
Chapter 6:	Sources of finance	78
	Template 5: Choosing sources of finance	87
Chapter 7:	The concept of trade credit	88
Chapter 8:	Cash flow, break-even and income statement	92
	Template 6: Projected income and expenditure	102
Chapter 9:	Marketing	103

Section 3: Implementing your enterprise project — 116

Chapter 10:	Negotiation	117
Chapter 11:	Communication	130
	Template 7: Planning and holding effective meetings	146
Chapter 12:	Help and support for enterprise	148

Section 4: Evaluating your enterprise project — 158

Chapter 13:	Evaluation	159

Glossary	182
Index	187
Acknowledgements	192

Introduction

This full-colour, illustrated coursebook has been written to support the latest Cambridge IGCSE® Enterprise (0454) syllabus, which will first be examined in 2020.

Written by experienced authors in clear, accessible language, this book is designed to be a practical guide to help build knowledge and understanding of the theoretical and practical aspects of setting up and running an enterprise and assumes no prior knowledge of the topics.

Syllabus and examination

The Cambridge IGCSE® Enterprise syllabus will help you to develop the skills needed for the work environment and for running a small business. Among other things, you'll learn about business planning, markets and customers, negotiation and the financial management. Assessment for this syllabus consists of one written exam paper and a coursework project. Each part counts for half your final grade. The exam paper consists of short answer, structured and open-ended questions which relate to what you have studied during the course as a whole, your coursework project and a pre-released case study. For the coursework project, you will need to provide a portfolio of evidence which demonstrates tasks undertaken as part of your enterprise project.

The book provides support for tackling both the exam paper and coursework project. Exam-style questions are included at the end of each chapter and each case study finishes with a series of questions. Both sets of questions have been written to help you develop the skills needed to answer the questions in the exam paper linked with the pre-released case study. Project prompt boxes throughout the chapters link the theory to the coursework project.

How to use this book

The book has been split into four sections, each linked to a key stage when setting up an enterprise project. Each chapter then covers the relevant content of the syllabus. Chapter 13 provides extra support and practice for developing your analysis and evaluation skills and applying these to your coursework project.

Each chapter has a similar structure. A variety of features will help you focus on developing your enterprise skills:

How to use this book

Learning summary
The key learning objectives are provided at the beginning of each chapter, helping you to navigate your way through each enterprise topic.

> ## Learning summary:
>
> **In this chapter you will learn about:**
> - the meaning of enterprise
> - stakeholders
> - enterprise capability
> - different ways of being enterprising at home and at school.

Key terms
Definitions help identify and understand important enterprise terminology and concepts.

> **KEY TERM**
>
> **Co-operative:** A type of business organisation that is owned and managed by people who use its services or who work there.

Activities
A range of individual and group learning activities are given within each chapter to develop knowledge and understanding.

> **ACTIVITY 9.1**
>
> What do you understand by the term marketing and why it is used? Write down your ideas. Share them with the person next to you. Are your ideas the same or different? Why do you think this? Are there more words you can add to your list? Share your ideas with another group.
> As a group, produce your definition of marketing and a list of reasons why it is used.

Project prompts
These help you apply the theory you are learning to the coursework tasks within your enterprise project.

> **PROJECT PROMPT**
>
> Whether you are working individually or as part of a group, try to create your own examples of different marketing communication for your enterprise project.
> Although the examples are not assessed, they can still be used as evidence of skills, such as creativity, or commented on when evaluating marketing communications used.

Tips
Tips provide additional context, reminders and useful information about key points.

> **TIP**
>
> In the presentation, you will be assessed on your enterprise and communication skills. You may want to be creative in how you do your presentation. Make sure you practise how and what you are going to say beforehand. This can also help you be less nervous when you do the actual presentation.

How to use this book

Case studies

Short studies from real-life enterprises illustrate how enterprise skills are used in practice. Questions help develop your analysis skills which could be applied to the pre-released case study.

> **MINI CASE STUDY**
>
> **P&N's Pens**
>
> Natalia and Paolo planned to sell stationery for their project.
>
> *The poster was more effective than using social media. Everyone who came to our stall said they knew about us from seeing the posters around school. Having obtained permission to use the school notice boards was helpful. This meant few posters were torn down which increased the potential number of people seeing them, and therefore lead to more people visiting our stall.*

Exam-style questions

Exam-style questions help you familiarise yourself with the style of the questions that you may come across, and assess your understanding and skills to answer them.

> **Exam-style questions**
>
> 1. State one advantage and one disadvantage of a partnership. [2]
> 2. What type of a business organisation is your enterprise? Explain two of its main features. [4]
> 3. In the McDonald's case study above, identify two stakeholders and explain their involvement in the enterprise. [4]
> 4. Describe the different stages of the enterprise process. [6]
> 5. With reference to your own enterprise, explain the importance of planning in the enterprise process. [6]
> 6. Compare and contrast the characteristics of a sole trader and a limited company. [10]

Summary

Each chapter ends with points that summarise the learning.

> **Summary**
>
> *You should know:*
>
> - the six stages in the enterprise process: identification of problem/need, exploring different solutions, action planning, implementing the plan, monitoring and evaluating success and failures
> - sole traders, partnerships, limited companies, franchises and co-operatives are different types of business organisation that exist to maximise profit for the owners. Each has their own legal status, advantages and disadvantages.
> - social enterprises work for the benefit of the community and not for the maximisation of the owners' profit
> - charities and not-for-profit organisations are examples of social enterprises.

Dear learner,

Welcome to the world of enterprise. You are taking the first steps in learning about one of the most important activities shaping our world – setting up and running new enterprises.

People undertake the founding of new enterprises for a variety of reasons:

- to provide the world (or some people in it) with new and exciting products and services
- to solve problems faced by people, communities and other enterprises
- to work for themselves, rather than for someone else
- to create something bigger than themselves
- to make a living.

Changes in technology, especially the development of the internet, have made it easier and less expensive than ever before to set up an enterprise. We can reach people who might like to work with or for our enterprise, or buy our products or services more easily and cheaply than enterprises ever could before. That means that more people, from all backgrounds, are taking the step of setting up enterprises – it's now a normal part of many people's careers and working lives, not an exceptional thing that only certain special people do.

You might be surprised to know that enterprise skills can help you in your further education. Any time there is a problem to be solved, one potential way to solve it, and bring people together, is to start an enterprise which focuses on solving that problem. For example, new ways to solve scientific or technical problems can be spread throughout the world by selling the new method for solving the problem to the people who have that problem. Or, if you notice that your friends or classmates have a particular problem, you may consider setting up an enterprise to help them make their lives easier or better.

More and more, people who come up with new ways to solve problems want to work with people who have enterprise skills to help them bring those solutions to the world. For example, when the computer engineer Steve Wozniak invented the first Apple personal computer, it was only with the help of Steve Jobs that he was able to find ways to get this new way of solving problems into people's hands. And when governments and large companies are trying to improve the

Foreword

way they do things, nowadays they often turn to people with enterprise skills and ask them to try to find new ways of working. In your community, people who have skills that could provide a service to others, or products that people could enjoy, might choose to team up with someone who has enterprise skills to help them provide those services or products through a new enterprise.

In this book, you will learn how to create and run an enterprise step by step. From thinking about different ideas for your enterprise to dealing with the legal aspects, planning the enterprise, dealing with money and making sure that your enterprise can sustain itself into the future by being profitable, finding customers, negotiating, managing people, and evaluating and controlling your enterprise, each step in the process is explained, and if you learn these steps, then you will have the tools to set up and run a simple but effective enterprise.

Enjoy learning about the challenges and skills of enterprise!

Dr Chris Coleridge
Senior Faculty in Management Practice
Cambridge Judge Business School
University of Cambridge

1

Introduction to enterprise

Learning summary:

In this chapter you will learn about:

- the meaning of enterprise
- stakeholders
- enterprise capability
- different ways of being enterprising at home and at school.

Introduction to enterprise

What is enterprise?

Enterprise is another word for an organisation or business managed by one or more individuals who are able to take the initiative to make decisions and take calculated risks. All business activities use resources like land, labour, capital and enterprise to produce goods and services that people want to buy.

Enterprise also refers to the characteristics/qualities that make people want to set up and run a business. It is the ability to be innovative, take initiative, make decisions and bear the risk of setting up and running a business.

Purpose and characteristics of enterprise

There are mainly two types of enterprise: business and social.

A **business enterprise**'s main aim is to make a profit. Any profits that are generated are reinvested into the business to grow it further or distributed to its owners/shareholders.

While the purpose of most enterprises is to make profits, there are some organisations that are started up for social causes, for the improvement of society and are not-for-profit. These are known as **social enterprises**. A social enterprise may generate profits, but that is not its main aim and profits are just seen as a way to sustain itself. Any profits made by a social enterprise are reinvested into things that benefit the community (see Chapter 1).

> **KEY TERMS**
>
> **Enterprise:** An organisation or business managed by one or more individuals who are able to take the initiative to make decisions and take calculated risks.
>
> **Business Enterprise:** An organisation that has profit as its main aim.
>
> **Social Enterprise:** An organisation that is started up for social cause for the betterment of society.

Enterprise capability

An **entrepreneur** is a person who starts up a new business or enterprise. Entrepreneurs are self-driven and innovative individuals who have a new idea for a good or service.

> **KEY TERMS**
>
> **Entrepreneur:** A person who starts up a new business or enterprise.
>
> **Stakeholder:** An individual, group or organisation with an interest in the activities of a business.

Entrepreneurs need to be multiskilled, self-confident, initiators, leaders and results-driven.

The key attributes that comprise enterprise capability are:

- **Risk-taking:** Though entrepreneurs recognise the risk of failure, it is the possibility of high returns and belief in themselves and their new idea that enable them to take a calculated risk. A calculated risk is a risk that is taken with an expectation that potential returns will be a lot more than the possible losses.

- **Decision-making:** Entrepreneurs should make sure they use the available resources in the best possible way and thus have to make decisions wisely. Decision-making and risk-taking are related as making a decision can involve many risks. Every time a decision is made there is a risk of losing the factors of production as well as the possible cost of not having used these resources in a more successful way.

- **Innovation:** While entrepreneurs can introduce a totally new product or service when setting up a new business, innovative entrepreneurs can spot opportunities for enterprise in existing products or services. They can do this by rebranding an existing product or a service and presenting it in a different way or in a different location or market.

- **Positive attitude:** A positive attitude is what drives entrepreneurs towards taking risks and facing and overcoming challenges.

Stakeholders

An entrepreneur who starts up a business may be the main owner, but there are many other **stakeholders**. A stakeholder is an individual, group or organisation with an interest in the activities of a business. An entrepreneur should make decisions with the interest of all stakeholders in mind. Stakeholders can be internal (directly involved with the running of the company) or external (outside parties that can affect and be affected by the business). Figure 0.1 shows the main stakeholders in an enterprise.

Introduction to enterprise

> **TIP**
>
> Never dismiss an idea as being too simple or not good enough. Always give it a go and find out how you can develop it further.

The main stakeholders in an enterprise

```
                              ┌── Employees
                  ┌─ Internal ┤
                  │           └── Owners/shareholders
                  │
                  │           ┌── Customers/consumers
                  │           │
                  │           ├── Government
Stakeholders ─────┤           │
                  │           ├── Local community
                  └─ External ┤
                              ├── Suppliers
                              │
                              ├── Lenders
                              │
                              └── Competition
```

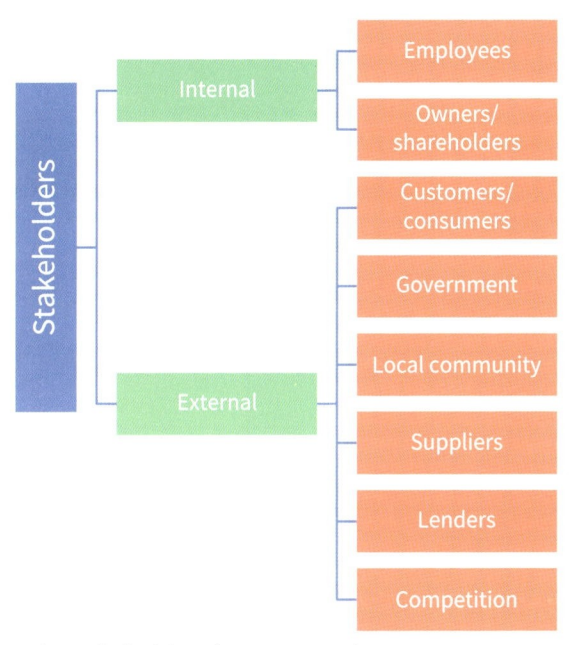

Figure 0.1: The main stakeholders in an enterprise

Employees: Employees are the people who do the work in an enterprise and earn a living from the operations of a business. To keep employees happy and productive an enterprise must provide them with fair wages, job security and good working conditions.

Owners/shareholders: Having invested in the enterprise, owners and shareholders want the business to grow and make profits. Healthy profits and the growth of an enterprise are important to attract further investment.

Customers/consumers: It is very important for an enterprise to satisfy its customers as they generate revenue for them by buying their products or services. To have a stable and loyal customer base an enterprise should provide a good quality product/service at a fair price.

Government: All businesses and individuals have to pay taxes to the government. In order to be law abiding and benefit from possible government grants and subsidies, an enterprise should follow all tax, labour and environmental laws. The government of a country is also interested in the employment generated by the operations of a business.

Local community: These are the people who live in the area near the business. They are affected by the impact that the business activity has on traffic, pollution and infrastructure in the area. In order to avoid complaints and opposition, an enterprise should aim to keep its negative impact to a minimum. The local community, on the other hand, can also gain from the infrastructural developments and jobs created by businesses in their area.

Suppliers: These are the businesses that supply the raw materials/products needed by an enterprise. They should be paid on time in order to ensure a timely and continuous supply of the needed supplies.

Lenders: These are the people or organisations that lend money to an enterprise, such as banks, other financial institutions and investors. It is important for an enterprise to repay the lenders on time so that they can borrow from them in the future.

Competition: These are businesses that operate in the same industry providing a similar product or service, targeting the same market. A business can both affect and be affected by the actions of its competition. To gain market share, an enterprise can set marketing and pricing strategies in line with (or even better than) that of the competition.

Introduction to enterprise

Ways of being enterprising at home and at school

Being enterprising at home

Organising a task:
being in charge of a meal, from buying food to cleaning up
laundry
shopping

Taking responsibility:
babysitting younger children
helping siblings with homework
feeding pets on time
exercising and grooming pets

Earning money:
babysitting
delivering newspapers
selling paintings/ art work

Organising yourself:
for a school trip
for a family picnic
finishing assignments on time

Being enterprising at school

Taking responsibility:
class monitoring
school prefect
class representative
team member or captain
buddying

Organising yourself:
getting to school on time
correct books
using a diary/school planner
handing in assignments on time

Leadership:
leading school clubs
running school sports events
setting up projects and campaigns

Earning money:
organising and running chairty fundraising events

Developing wider enterprising skills

Applying technology:
revision websites and apps
web storage mechanisms to share information

Building communication and numeracy skills:
analysing data
applying logic and reasoning
verbal/non-verbal skills to get your point across

Thinking creatively and independently:
new solutions to problems
creative solutions as a team
out-of-the-box approach

Learning independently/ as a group:
identify your strengths/ weaknesses
good speaker
good listener
learn from others mistakes and experience

Reasoned evaluations:
compare
analyse
evaluate
choose the best option

Figure 0.2: Ways of being enterprising

KEY TERMS

Analyse: Examine in detail to show meaning, identify elements and the relationship between them.

Evaluate: Judge or calculate the quality, importance, amount, or value of something.

Identify: Name/select/recognise.

Explain: Set out purposes or reasons/make the relationships between things evident/provide why and/or how and support with relevant evidence.

ACTIVITY 0.1

Think of yourself as a social entrepreneur and identify a need or challenge faced by your school or community, and develop ideas to solve it.

An example of a challenge faced by a school might be the shortage of funds to buy enough computers and sports equipment. You could run an event to raise awareness of or raise funds for your cause. Remember the different ways of being enterprising discussed earlier.

1. What initiatives/different fundraising events could the different stakeholders (such as the school, students and parents) take part in to solve this challenge?
2. What do you think the different stakeholders have to gain from helping your school raise funds?

TIP

Make sure your spoken and written communication is simple and clear.

PROJECT PROMPT

- What is the aim of your enterprise?
- Will your enterprise be a social or profit-making enterprise?
- Identify and explain the role of the external stakeholders in your enterprise.
- Identify some ways in which you can be enterprising to make your enterprise project a success.

MINI CASE STUDY

Nirali Someshwar, India

An architect by qualification but with a passion for dance, today Ms Nirali Someshwar is an entrepreneur. She has successfully run her dance academy Happy Feet in Pune and Mumbai, India for the last 10 years. The setup of this creative enterprise was completely unplanned: she performed at a few festivals and events but her great performances immediately attracted a group of parents who wanted her to train their children. She decided to pursue her passion and took the initiative to set up her academy. With effort, dedication and planning she began classes at five different locations in Pune, India. Happy Feet teaches various forms of Indian and Western dance and does choreography for various school and corporate events and weddings. With art and dance gaining popularity and becoming a mainstream profession, there is a lot of competition in this industry. However, Nirali feels her love for what she does, her determination and hard work will help her expand further.

Questions:

1. Identify the different ways in which Nirali Someshwar has been enterprising.
2. How can she continue to be enterprising in order to face the challenges of a competitive industry?
3. What risk factors do you think she may have considered before taking the decision to set up her dance academy?
4. Identify the different stakeholders of the enterprise.
5. With reference to this case study, explain whether this is a business or a social enterprise. Outline the difference between a social and a business enterprise.

Summary

You should know:

- the two main types of enterprise: a social enterprise (not-for-profit) and a business enterprise (where the aim is to make a profit)
- making well-thought-out decisions, being innovative and taking risks are the three main characteristics of an enterprise
- entrepreneurs who start up an enterprise have to be mindful of the interests of all stakeholders
- stakeholders are people and organisations that have an interest in the activity of a business. They can be internal (within the organisation) or external (outside of the organisation). Employees and shareholders are internal stakeholders, whereas lenders and suppliers are some examples of external stakeholders.
- you can be enterprising in everything you do at home and at school by taking more initiative and responsibility and being organised and creative.

Learning summary

In this chapter you will learn about:
- the different stages of the enterprise process
- the key points to consider at each stage
- the characteristics of different types of business organisations.

The enterprise process

To be successful in an enterprise activity, an enterprising person needs to follow various steps in order. This is called the **enterprise process**. Make sure you consider each of these steps as you plan and implement your own enterprise project.

> **KEY TERM**
>
> **Enterprise process:** The various stages involved in starting and running an enterprise.

Identifying the problem, need or want → Exploring creative solutions → Action planning → Implementing the plan → Monitoring progress → Evaluation of successes and failures

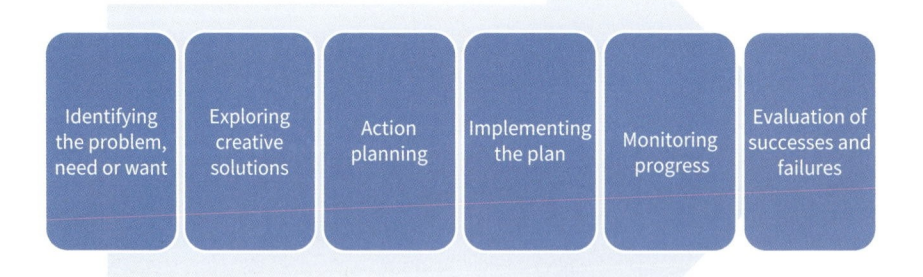

Figure 1.1: The enterprise process

Identifying the problem, need or want:
- A combination of group discussion, brain storming and individual reflection should be used to identify and understand the problem, need or want. Collecting ideas and thoughts from different people involved/stakeholders will ensure many different aspects of the business opportunity have been considered.
- A suitable risk assessment needs to be carried out before starting an enterprise activity.
- The identification of the enterprise opportunity/idea should be backed up with thorough research about the market need. This helps the enterprise have a clear aim and vision that it can work towards. The expected rate of return if it is to be a business enterprise, should also be considered.

Chapter 1: Setting up a new enterprise

- Recognition of the skills required and reflection on whether an entrepreneur and his associates have them is important for the success of the enterprise. If there are any skills gaps then there should be a plan in place to fill them.

Exploring creative solutions
- When aiming to solve a problem or meet a need, creative and innovative ways need to be looked at and evaluated. Creativity and innovation are key traits of a successful enterprise. They help entrepreneurs find new ways of solving existing problems and meeting needs.
- These creative ideas then need to be analysed and evaluated to help choose the most effective solution. Mind maps can be used to explore the links between ideas which can then be very helpful in developing an effective enterprise plan.

Action planning:
- This involves, making plans for the enterprise activity keeping the costs, budget and financial capability in mind.
- Breaking down goals into achievable tasks.
- Using resources and team members most efficiently. Allocating roles according to people's strengths, skills and attributes to increase the chances of success.
- Setting appropriate timescales and milestones, working towards the goals set out earlier.

Implementing the plan
- To be successful, enterprise activities must be carried out efficiently, effectively, lawfully and with due regard to health and safety.
- All milestones, timescales and health and safety issues identified in the plan should be frequently referred to. This ensures that the activities and tasks are focused and directed towards meeting objectives.
- Things don't always work out as planned and unexpected events do happen. In such a case, decision-making needs to be quick, flexible and responsive.

Monitoring Progress
- Constantly monitoring and evaluating progress against the objectives set out is a way to make sure that projects are tracked and any deviations identified.

- If tasks are not done and objectives not met on time, corrective action/adjustments need to be done in response to any deviations from the plan. This is essential to ensure that objectives are met and goals achieved within the allocated budget and time.

Evaluation of successes and failures
- This involves reviewing the final outcomes against achievement criteria. This is done in order to draw lessons from the activity and come up with suggestions for improvement in the future.
- Skills, attitudes, qualities, understanding acquired and lessons learned should also be assessed and reflected on to enhance the success of future enterprise projects or activities.

TIP
Word processing and spreadsheet software tools can be very useful for recording ideas and plans, and for creating timelines for target setting and monitoring.

Putting data and figures into tables makes it easier to understand the information. Use a spreadsheet to store information and perform calculations.

ACTIVITY 1.1
Your group has been given the task of starting a new club in school. Brainstorm for ideas with your team. Some examples of new clubs that could be offered are:
- helping children in the lower classes with maths/science/English
- sports club offering a popular or sport of your choice
- debating club.

Once you have decided on which club your group will be starting, discuss all the things you need to consider to get it running. Consider the various stages of the enterprise process and what you need to do. You can make an enterprise process mind map or make a list of the points.

1. Which club has your group decided to start? How did you identify this club as the best one to start?
2. What planning do you need to do in order to start the club? One of the things to think about is the venue where the club will meet. What other things should be considered?
3. How will you implement the plans that you have made?
4. How will you ensure that your club is running successfully?

Chapter 1: Setting up a new enterprise

PROJECT PROMPT

As you start your enterprise project, have an overview about how your project will develop through various stages of the enterprise process

1. When identifying the problem/need of your project, identify the various factors that you will have to consider. Think about the research you will have to do to make informed decisions. What will be the aim/vision of your enterprise? Consider the risks involved in starting and running your enterprise.
2. Analyse how the solution that you have found to the need/problem identified in your project is the most creative and effective.
3. When making your action plan, think of all the financial and marketing aspects of your enterprise.
4. Find out about all sources of help and support from the government and other organisations that you could use.
5. Think about what milestones you might set to be able to monitor the progress of your project.
6. At each stage, remember to reflect on what worked well and what could have been improved.

Types of business organisations

Businesses may be organised in many different ways, each with its own legal status, advantages and disadvantages.

Types of business organisations:
- Sole trader
- Limited company
  - Private limited
  - Public limited
- Partnership
- Co-operative
- Social enterprise
  - Charities
  - Not-for-profit
- Franchise

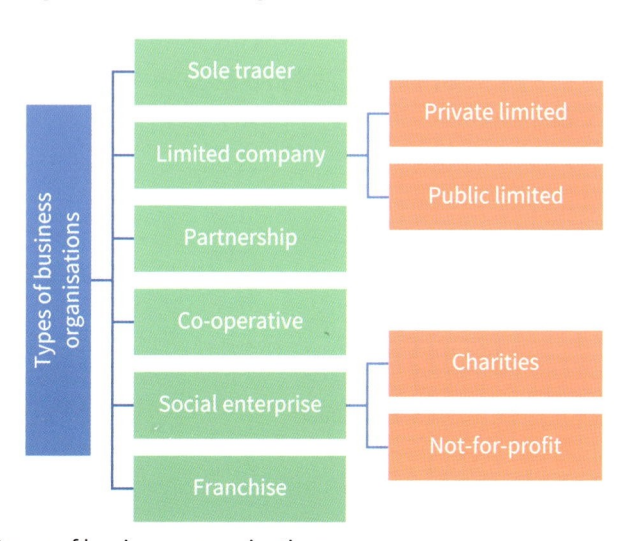

Figure 1.2: Types of business organisations

Sole trader

This is a business that is owned and run by just one person though it may employ staff. A **sole trader** is an **unincorporated business**. This means it is not a separate entity from the owner. The owner has **unlimited liability** and is liable for all the debts of the business and stands to lose his/her investment as well as personal assets if the business goes into debt. However, this is one of the most common types of business organisations, mainly because it is cheaper and simpler to start. Examples include hairdressers, photographers, freelance writers and artists.

> **KEY TERMS**
>
> **Sole trader:** A business that is owned and run by just one person though it may employ staff. It is an unincorporated business in which the owner has unlimited liability for all the debts of the business.
>
> **Unincorporated business:** A business that does not possess a separate legal identity from its owner. The owner(s) have full liability for the business.
>
> **Unlimited liability:** Shareholders/owners are liable for all the debts of their organisation and stand to lose their investment as well as personal assets if the business goes into debt.

Advantages of being a sole trader:
- Cheap, quick and simple (less documentation and legal formalities) to start.
- The owner can keep all the profits.
- The owner can make his/her own decisions and has full control of their business.

Disadvantages of being a sole trader:
- The owner is fully responsible for all debt, also known as unlimited liability
- It is difficult to raise finance, so often the owner has to rely on personal savings.

Partnerships

This is a business that is owned by two or more people, who are known as the partners. **Partnerships** cannot normally have more than 20 partners though this can vary from country to country. This sort of a business organisation is also unincorporated and so the partners have unlimited liability. Lawyers, accountants and small businesses owned by two or more people are usually set up as partnerships.

> **KEY TERM**
>
> **Partnership:** A business that is owned by two or more people, known as the partners. This sort of a business organisation is unincorporated and so the partners have unlimited liability.

Chapter 1: Setting up a new enterprise

Advantages of partnerships:
- Cheap, quick and simple (less documentation and legal formalities) to start.
- The partners can keep all the profits.
- The partners have full control of their business.
- The decision-making and workload is shared.

Disadvantages of partnerships:
- The partners are fully responsible for all debt (also known as unlimited liability).
- It is difficult to raise finance, so often entrepreneurs have to rely on personal savings.
- Disagreements and conflicts between partners can slow down the business.
- The decision made by one partner is legally binding on all the others.

Limited companies

Limited companies are incorporated businesses that are a separate legal entity from their owners. A limited company is owned by its shareholders who own a share of the company. There are two types of limited companies.

Private limited company
The shares of a private limited company are usually held by friends and family so there are a small number of shareholders.

Public limited company
Shares are offered to and often owned by the public and other organisations.

Advantages of a limited company:
- The shareholders have a **limited liability**, which means they are not fully liable for the debts of the business. Shareholders/owners are only liable to pay/lose the amount they have invested.
- It is easier to raise finance than it is for sole traders and partnerships as they can sell their company's shares.

> **KEY TERMS**
>
> **Limited company:** An incorporated business that is a separate legal entity from its owners.
>
> **Limited liability:** Shareholders/owners are only liable to pay or lose the amount they have invested.

- Since the company is a separate unit from the owners, it will continue to exist even if one of the owners leaves or dies.

Disadvantages of a limited company:
- Limited companies are not so easy to set up as there are a lot of legal formalities, rules and regulations to be followed.
- The original owners may lose control of the business as shares are sold to the public.
- The accounts of the company have to be published for the public to see.

Co-operatives

This type of business organisation is owned and managed by people who use its services and who work there. There are different types of **co-operative**.

> **KEY TERM**
>
> **Co-operative:** A type of business organisation that is owned and managed by people who use its services or who work there.

- A consumer co-operative is owned by consumers who buy its goods or services.
- A producer co-operative is owned by producers of goods who have come together to sell their goods.
- A worker co-operative is one which is run by its employees.

Advantages of co-operatives:
- Co-operatives are democratic.
- The members (whether consumers or employees) work together. There are fewer chances of conflict as members share a common interest.
- The owners/shareholders in a co-operative usually have limited liability.
- Co-operatives usually get some sort of tax relief from the government.
- Most co-operatives are treated as separate legal units and so the death of a member does not affect its continuity.

Disadvantages of co-operatives:
- It is difficult to raise finance as co-operatives cannot issue shares.
- Accounts have to be made accessible to the public.
- Members may not necessarily have the required skills to run the business and so have to hire professionals who may be expensive.

Franchises

A **franchise** is a form of business organisation that allows a company (franchisee) to buy the right to use an existing company's (franchisor) brand name and products/service. For example, Subway, the sandwich shop opened its first franchise in Connecticut, USA in 1965. Other Subway franchises soon followed and now there are more Subway restaurants in the world than any other restaurant chain.

> **KEY TERM**
>
> **Franchise:** A form of business organisation that allows a company (franchisee) to buy the right to use an existing company's (franchisor) brand name and products/service.

Advantages of franchises:
- The franchisee has a greater chance of success as they are selling a well-known product/service.
- The franchisor may provide some support to the franchisee by providing advice and training.
- The franchisor may contribute funds or do some advertising at national level, reducing the franchisee's costs.
- Easier to gain loans from bank, as the business is seen to be low-risk.

Disadvantages of franchises:
- The franchisee will have to pay a license fee and possibly a percentage of the revenue to the franchisor.
- The initial costs of setting up a franchise business may be high.
- The franchisee will not have full control over how he can run his business as he will have to follow the controls set by the franchisor.

Social enterprises

A social enterprise is a business with social objectives and ethical values aimed at benefitting the community. The money earned is reinvested in the business or used for a social cause. There are different types of social enterprise.

Not-for-profit enterprises
- Not-for-profit enterprises are directly involved in producing goods or providing services, but in a socially responsible way.
- They often sell products or services in order to reinvest their profits into the business for the benefit of the community and not-for-profit maximisation of its owners/shareholders.

- They generate their own income and do not rely on donations to survive.
- A not-for-profit organisation's aim is to improve social conditions. The aims may be short-term or may last for decades.

> **KEY TERM**
>
> **Income:** All the money that comes in to an enterprise.

Charities
- Charities raise money by doing fundraising activities and collecting donations.
- Charities work to provide quick solutions to immediate disasters/adversity and their impact is often short lived.

Advantages of social enterprises:
- Committed employees: employees who work for a social enterprise often feel for the cause and have a personal interest in its social aims and objectives.
- Job satisfaction for employees is high as they know they have made a difference to people in need.
- They bring about a positive change to people and communities.

Disadvantages of social enterprises:
- Social enterprises may be less competitive in the market due to limited capital.

> **TIP**
>
> Consider your skills and personality when deciding what type of organisation your enterprise will be.

> **ACTIVITY 1.2**
>
> In a group, research and discuss an enterprise that has come up internationally or in your own country recently. You may use the internet or a business magazine/journal for your research. What type of an organisation is it? What is the main product/service offered by the enterprise? What are the risk factors/challenges faced by the enterprise? Is it successful so far?

> **PROJECT PROMPT**
>
> What type of a business organisation will best suit your enterprise? Explain why you think this sort of organisation will be best suited to you.
>
> It isn't a requirement for the coursework, but it would still be useful to think about which type of organisation will best suit your enterprise.
>
> What are the disadvantages of this sort of organisation and how could you minimise them?

Chapter 1: Setting up a new enterprise

MINI CASE STUDY

Betty Makoni, Zimbabwe

Having suffered abuse as a child, Betty Makoni founded the Girl Child Network Zimbabwe in 1998. It started as an informal discussion group/club in a classroom. Its main aim was to allow girls a safe space to meet and talk freely about their problems and find possible solutions. In collaboration with the social services department and other government regulatory bodies, it is now at the forefront of identifying and tackling abuse and has mentored thousands of girls around Zimbabwe. Its model is being used in other parts of Africa and it has grown into an international charity, Girl Child Network Worldwide. It is a not-for-profit organisation with the social aim to protect and promote the rights of girls all over the world.

Questions:

1. What characteristics of the Girl Child Network make it a social enterprise?
2. Using the case study, explain the main differences between a sole trader and a social enterprise.
3. What do you think are the main challenges faced by a social enterprise like the Girl Child Network?
4. What do you think are the driving factors behind people working for such an enterprise?

Richard and Maurice McDonald, USA

The McDonald brothers, Richard and Maurice, opened their first restaurant in 1940 in San Bernardino, California as a barbecue restaurant focused on quality and quick service. Having spotted its potential to expand throughout the United States and beyond, Ray Kroc joined the company in 1954. He grew the business by offering franchises. There are now more than 29 000 McDonald's restaurants in over 120 countries and it is one of the largest food service companies in the world.

McDonald's, the franchisor, grants the right to sell McDonald's branded goods to someone wishing to set up their own business: the franchisee. To ensure consistent quality standards across all McDonald's restaurants all franchisees have to use standardised McDonald's branding, menus, design layouts and administrative systems. McDonald's also provides the franchisees with initial training, continuous support and coordinated marketing. For the franchising to be a success there is a special three-way relationship that exists between McDonalds, the franchisee and the suppliers.

Using franchising as a means to expand has proven to be very beneficial for McDonald's as franchises bring entrepreneurs, full of determination and ideas, into the organisation along with a monthly rent. Responding to local consumer tastes, many new items on McDonald's menus have come from franchisees.

The role of the supplier is critical to the success of the franchise operation. As McDonald's considers the quality of its products to be of absolute importance, it sets very high standards for its suppliers and believes in developing close relationships with them. Suppliers who have been able to meet McDonald's standards have been able to share in the growth and success of McDonald's.

Chapter 1: Setting up a new enterprise

Questions:
1. Discuss the main advantages to a business entering the restaurant industry either by buying a franchise or opening a restaurant as a limited company.
2. Discuss the challenges that may be faced by a McDonald's franchisee.
3. What are some of the advantages to McDonald's when expanding by offering its franchises?
4. Explain the role and importance of suppliers as stakeholders in McDonald's.

Exam-style questions

1. State one advantage and one disadvantage of a partnership. [2]
2. What type of a business organisation is your enterprise? Explain two of its main features. [4]
3. In the McDonald's case study above, identify two stakeholders and explain their involvement in the enterprise. [4]
4. Describe the different stages of the enterprise process. [6]
5. With reference to your own enterprise, explain the importance of planning in the enterprise process. [6]
6. Compare and contrast the characteristics of a sole trader and a limited company. [10]

KEY TERMS

Describe: State the points of a topic/give characteristics and main features.
Discuss: Write about issue(s) or topic(s) in depth in a structured way.
State: Express in clear terms.

Summary

You should know:

- the six stages in the enterprise process: identification of problem/need, exploring different solutions, action planning, implementing the plan, monitoring and evaluating success and failures
- sole traders, partnerships, limited companies, franchises and co-operatives are different types of business organisation that exist to maximise profit for the owners. Each has their own legal status, advantages and disadvantages.
- social enterprises work for the benefit of the community and not for the maximisation of the owners' profit
- charities and not-for-profit organisations are examples of social enterprises.

Learning summary

In this chapter you will learn about:

- the skills of enterprising people
- your own enterprise skills
- how enterprising people have used their skills to be successful.

Skills of enterprising people

Enterprising people make the most of their **knowledge** and **skills** to be successful in what they aim to do. An enterprising person could be:

- someone in your school (for example, a learner who has successfully raised money for a charity)
- from the local community (for example, a person who has successfully set up a local small business)
- from the wider community (for example, a person who has successfully set up a national or multinational company).

> **KEY TERMS**
>
> **Knowledge:** The theoretical facts and information that you gather through your experience or education.
>
> **Skills:** Your ability to do something. This can be something that you were born with such as a natural ability to encourage and motivate people, or it could be something that you have learnt such as time management.

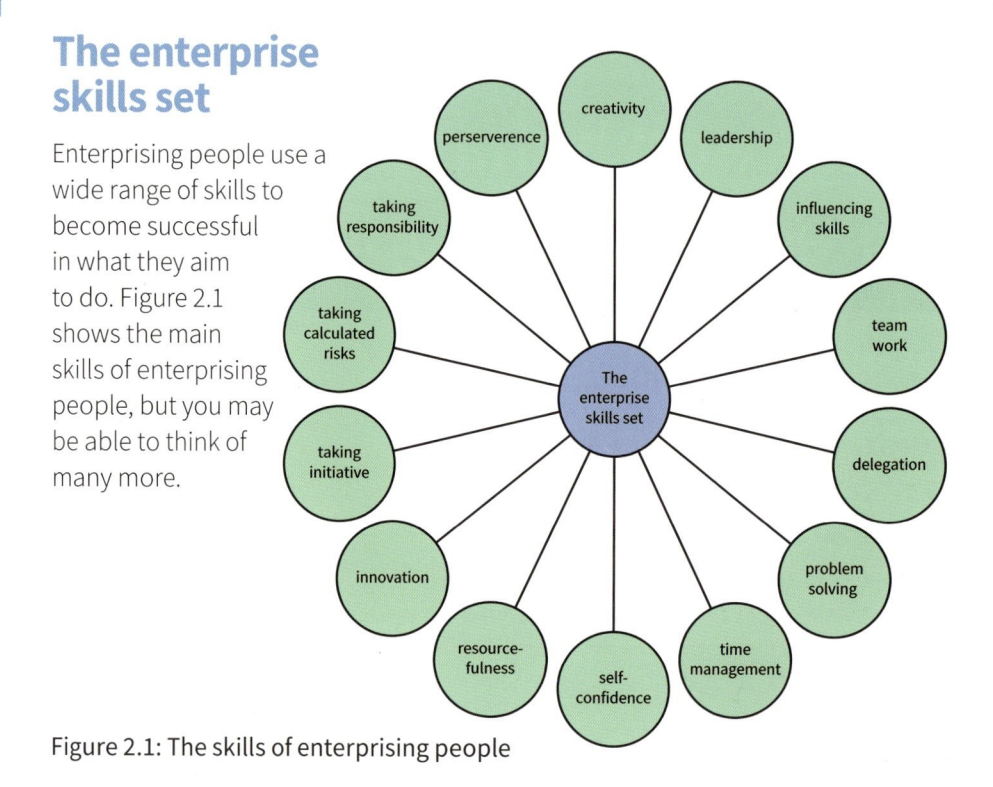

The enterprise skills set

Enterprising people use a wide range of skills to become successful in what they aim to do. Figure 2.1 shows the main skills of enterprising people, but you may be able to think of many more.

The enterprise skills set:
- creativity
- perserverence
- leadership
- taking responsibility
- influencing skills
- taking calculated risks
- team work
- taking initiative
- delegation
- innovation
- problem solving
- resource-fulness
- self-confidence
- time management

Figure 2.1: The skills of enterprising people

Chapter 2: Skills and behaviours of enterprising people

ACTIVITY 2.1

The following are some enterprise skills (in pink) and their definitions (in yellow). Write out the skills with the correct definition for each one.

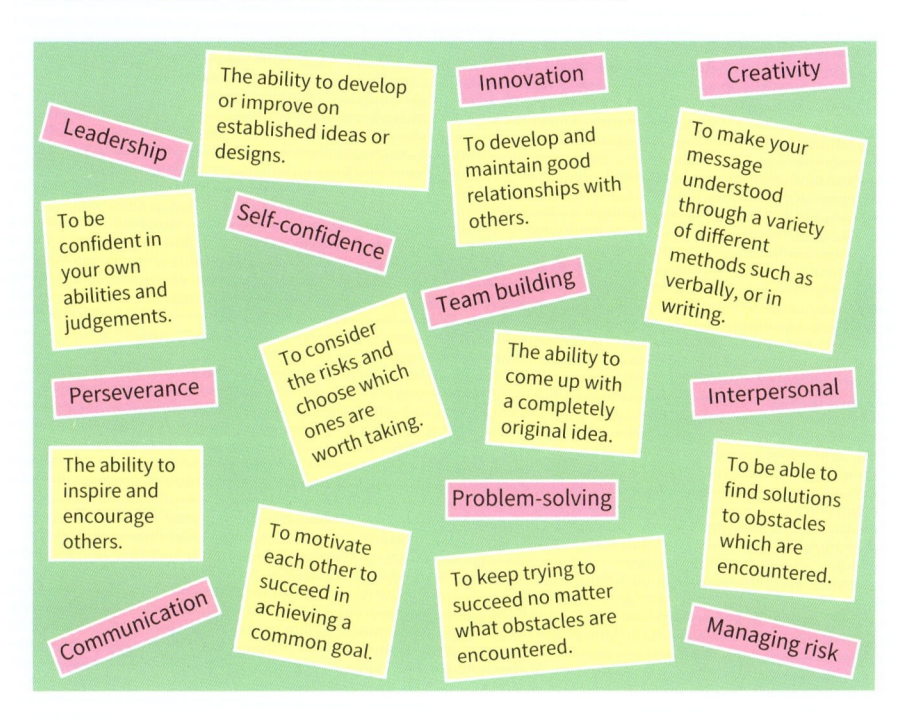

- **Innovation** — The ability to develop or improve on established ideas or designs.
- **Leadership** — The ability to inspire and encourage others.
- **Self-confidence** — To be confident in your own abilities and judgements.
- **Team building** — To develop and maintain good relationships with others.
- **Creativity** — The ability to come up with a completely original idea.
- **Communication** — To make your message understood through a variety of different methods such as verbally, or in writing.
- **Perseverance** — To keep trying to succeed no matter what obstacles are encountered.
- **Managing risk** — To consider the risks and choose which ones are worth taking.
- **Problem-solving** — To be able to find solutions to obstacles which are encountered.
- **Interpersonal** — To motivate each other to succeed in achieving a common goal.

MINI CASE STUDY

Arjun Santoth Kumar, India

Arjun travels to and from school on the school bus. One day a cyclone hit the city where Arjun lives causing disruption that meant his journey home took a very long time. By the time he got home his parents were very worried.

Arjun used his resourcefulness to innovate a simple product that would let parents track the travel progress of the school bus and receive alerts if the bus ran late. He created Ez School Bus Locator for which he won the Massachusetts Institute of Technology (MIT)'s App Inventor Contest in December 2013.

Since then Arjun has taken the calculated risk to set up his own company and, at 15 years of age, Arjun Santoth Kumar became CEO of his company, LateraLogics. The company makes custom apps for mobile phones and websites.

Questions:

1. Identify the three enterprise skills that Arjun used to make his enterprise a success.
2. Explain how you used one enterprise skill in your enterprise project.

ACTIVITY 2.2

In this activity you explore the skills you think are most important in an enterprising person. Draw a body outline (like the one shown) on a sheet of paper and label all the enterprise skills you think a successful enterprising person should have. Decide on the top 10 skills and then rank them in order of importance, 1 being the most important and 10 being the least important. When you have done this, have a discussion with your class to see if others had the same top 10 as you.

Following your discussion, draw a big outline on a large sheet of paper and agree as a class the top 10 enterprise skills.

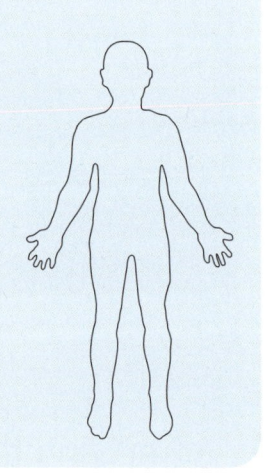

Identifying and evaluating enterprise skills

Even the most successful enterprising people were not born with a full set of enterprise skills! It is important that enterprising people know what their strong skills are as well their weaker ones, and which ones they simply do not have (yet). An enterprising person will often make good use of their strong skills to be successful. They will also work to improve the weaker skills, or learn new ones where they have gaps in their skills set. Sometimes they will work with other people with different enterprise skills to cover their weaker skills and gaps.

Chapter 2: Skills and behaviours of enterprising people

PROJECT PROMPT

For your enterprise project you will need to comment on the enterprise skills that you used when implementing your plan.

Skills audit

A skills audit is one way in which an enterprising person can identify the skills they do or do not have. Ideally, enterprising people will think about all the skills that they might need to use and honestly rate themselves from being strong at using a skill to not having that skill at all. They might also ask others to rate them in how strong or weak they are in those skills. When the audit is complete the enterprising person will be able to:

- identify their strong skills and consider how they will use their strengths to make the enterprise successful
- identify the weaknesses or gaps in their enterprise skills set and consider the potential risks to the enterprise from the weaknesses or gaps in their skills
- investigate how they could improve weak skills and address the gaps in skills.

ACTIVITY 2.3

The following table is a simple skills audit that focuses on the 10 skills you defined earlier in this chapter. Draw your own copy of the table. Think about when you have previously used these skills and how good you were at using each one. Rate yourself using the ratings given in the key.

Skill	Where you have previously demonstrated using this skill	Rating
Leadership		
Innovation		
Creativity		
Team building		
Managing risk		
Communication		
Interpersonal		

Perseverance		
Self-confidence		
Solving problems		

Key:

- Strong: Regularly demonstrates they are capable of using this skill
- Fair: Seen to use this skill occasionally
- Weak: Does not feel confident using this skill/needs to develop this skill

Behaviours of enterprising people

The previous section looked at the range of skills that enterprising people need. This section explores how enterprising people use those skills to be successful.

MINI CASE STUDY

Tanya Budd, United Kingdom

When Tanya was 17 years old she took a sailing course with friends. During the course she realised that there was a need for a better way to rescue a person who had fallen from the boat, a task that is especially difficult if the person who has fallen is unconscious. Tanya was studying design at school so, as part of her coursework, she created the Hypo-Hoist, a simple device to get people out of the water. For her creativity Tanya was named 'Young Engineer for Britain 2005/2006' and she was also awarded the 'US Coast Guard Award for Maritime Safety' in 2006.

To take the Hypo-Hoist from a design concept to a commercially viable product Tanya had to apply for a patent, get advice from specialists and finally have the product tested and approved. She also had to find a company to manufacture and distribute the product before organising an international launch at the Southampton Boat Show. Her Hypo-Hoist has been in commercial production since 2007. Tanya continues to use her knowledge and skills to improve on the Hypo-Hoist and other products.

Chapter 2: Skills and behaviours of enterprising people

Enterprise skills	In practice…	How Tanya Budd was enterprising
Creativity	… a person uses their imagination to improve on an already established idea or design.	Tanya used her creativity to develop a better way of getting an injured person out of the water and onto the boat/ship safely.
Perseverance	… a person continues to do something despite difficulty and setbacks.	Tanya tried numerous designs without success but kept going and finally came up with her award-winning design.
Initiative	… a person seizes opportunities to act or take charge.	Despite winning awards, Tanya did not expect companies to come to her and buy her design. She researched marine safety companies, took her product to them and persuaded one to make it.

ACTIVITY 2.4

Research an enterprising person in your local community and write a case study about them, like the one about Tanya Budd. You might include the following things:
- A short biography
- What was their childhood like? (When were they born? Were they rich or poor? What was their education like?)
- What was their big business break? (What business was it that this happened in? How did it happen?)
- What skills did they demonstrate in order to become successful?

ACTIVITY 2.5

Create a table like the one in Tanya Budd's case study for the enterprising person you have researched. In the first two columns list and define three skills that the enterprising person has used. In the third column, write a summary of how your chosen enterprising person used each skill.

KEY TERM

Define: Give precise meaning.

PROJECT PROMPT

In your project you will need to explain five of the skills that you have used in implementing your plan (one of which must be the skill of negotiation). To help you do this, keep a record of the skills you used and when throughout your project.

Exam-style questions

1 Using the case study on Tanya Budd, or an entrepreneur that you have investigated, describe how that person has successfully used two enterprise skills. [4]

2 Explain one way in which the following entrepreneurial skills might help make an enterprise successful: [4]

   - Problem-solving
   - Time management

3 Referring to examples of the enterprise skills you used in your enterprise project, discuss how you effectively used those enterprise skills to successfully complete your enterprise project. [15]

Summary

You should know:

- a range of key enterprise skills, including leadership, taking responsibility, negotiation, delegation, problem-solving, time management, resourcefulness, innovation, taking initiative and taking risks
- how to identify and evaluate your own skills
- how entrepreneurs use their enterprise skills.

Learning summary

In this chapter you will learn about:

- how opportunities arise
- the risks involved in enterprise
- the process of identifying, analysing and managing risks
- why laws and regulations to protect stakeholders exist and the impact of these laws and regulations
- how an enterprise may have an impact on communities and society
- ethical considerations within enterprise.

Enterprise opportunities

Setting up an enterprise involves risks and **rewards**. Part of being enterprising means identifying **opportunities** and being willing to take some element of risk in order to successfully develop the idea.

Many factors can create opportunities. These factors can be local, national, international or global, including:

> **KEY TERMS**
>
> **Reward:** Something given in recognition of effort or return for something achieved.
>
> **Opportunity:** A time or event that makes it possible to do something.

- changing needs or wants for a product or service, for example an increase or decrease in income, changes in taste and fashion, or changes in population size or structure
- developments in technology making new products and services possible and others out-dated or unwanted
- changes in the ability to meet needs or wants, for example the failure of competition or access to equipment
- changes in government policies including availability of grants and subsidies or changes in taxation and laws.

These factors will influence the level of demand as well as an enterprise's ability to meet that demand.

MINI CASE STUDY

Noa Mintz, USA; Benny Fajarai, Indonesia

The idea for a new enterprise can come from unexpected sources. For example:

- When Noa Mintz was 12 years old she didn't like her babysitter, so her mother set her a light-hearted challenge to find a better one for their family. She did, and then started helping her mother's friends to find babysitters for their children. (For more information see her website at www.nanniesbynoa.com).
- Benny Fajarai was visiting Bali when he noticed how much tourists liked the traditional Indonesian handicrafts. Benny was quick to realise the potential market demand and also saw an opportunity to help local craftspeople. Benny and a friend created Qlapa – an online marketplace for handmade goods.

Question:

Investigate other entrepreneurs. What opportunity did they see that resulted in them starting their enterprise?

Chapter 3: Opportunities, risk, legal and ethical considerations

> **TIP**
>
> Once you have identified an opportunity you should decide how to take advantage of it. Try to be creative when thinking about solutions.

> **PROJECT PROMPT**
>
> In your project you will need to explore two or three potential enterprise ideas. From these you need to choose one. There will be opportunities all around you, at home and at school. The ideas you choose can be as simple as selling food and drink at a school event, washing cars or setting up a fashion show. You (or your group) decide. What is important is that you consider ideas that are suitable and feasible for you to carry out.

Risks

Risk is part of life. However careful you try to be, no activity is completely safe.

> **KEY TERM**
>
> **Risk:** The chance of gaining or losing something as a result of an action taken.

Figure 3.1: Risks are a part of life

Risk-taking is a key characteristic of being a successful entrepreneur. Failure can happen to anyone. Mistakes are natural so do not be afraid try new ideas. If something does not work, learn from what went wrong and use the experience to help improve next time. Many famous entrepreneurs, including Bill Gates and Steve Jobs, had businesses that failed before they were successful.

Risks can be positive or negative. The decision to start up an enterprise or develop a new product may or may not work. For example:

- It is not certain to make a profit.
- Choosing the wrong pricing or promotion strategy can result in the loss of customers.
- Having too many unexpected customers can be just as much of a problem as having too few.

An entrepreneur will try to make decisions that give the best chance of ensuring rewards and reducing the potential for something to go wrong.

How to manage risk

Many enterprises will carry out a risk assessment as part of the planning process to identify and assess possible risks involved in a project or activity.

An enterprise must deal with many possible risks, including:

- Financial risks, e.g. having access to sufficient finance or what to do about unexpected costs.
- Economic risks, e.g. what to do about changes in income, customer tastes or interest rates.
- Health and safety and environmental risks, e.g. how laws and regulations affect what or how you operate.
- Human resource risks, e.g. having the right skills and number of people in the enterprise.
- Production risks, e.g. access to the right materials, or what to do if a machine breaks down.

Not all of these points will apply to every enterprise or situation. By knowing the risks they will face the entrepreneur can plan properly, using the information to make decisions about what action to take (or not) about each risk. This means the enterprise has a better chance of achieving its objectives.

Chapter 3: Opportunities, risk, legal and ethical considerations

ACTIVITY 3.1

Imagine you have been asked to organise a school trip or an end-of-year party for your class.

Identify possible risks that you might to deal with when organising the event.

TIP

You will not be asked to complete a risk assessment for your enterprise project.

The stages of risk management

Figure 3.1 shows you the stages of risk management.

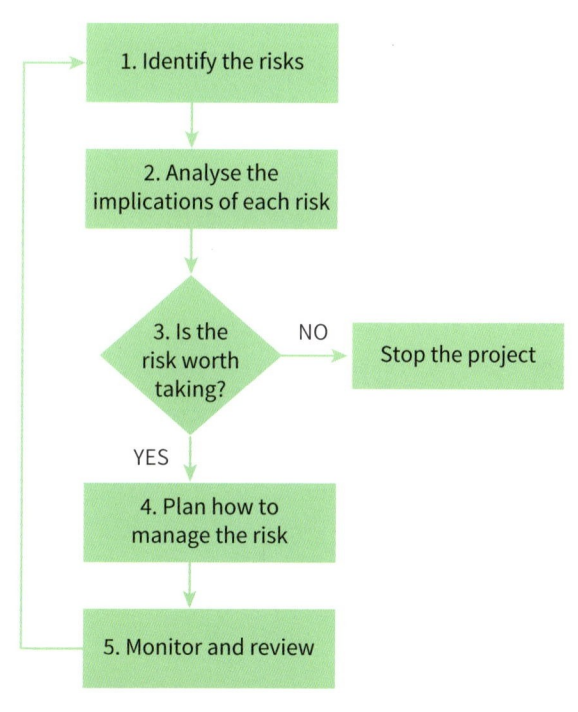

```
1. Identify the risks
        ↓
2. Analyse the
implications of each risk
        ↓
3. Is the risk worth taking?  ──NO──▶  Stop the project
        │
       YES
        ↓
4. Plan how to manage the risk
        ↓
5. Monitor and review
```

Figure 3.2: The stages of risk management

Step 1: Identify the risk

PEST and SWOT are two methods that can be used to collect information to help identify relevant external or internal factors that may represent possible risks.

PEST analysis

This involves identifying important external factors that could have an impact on an enterprise. These are factors that affect the whole market and the enterprise has no control over them. External factors also form the basis for Opportunities and Threats in a SWOT analysis.

Factors to consider include:

Political factors	Economic factors
Political stability	Inflation
Taxation	Interest rates
Legal controls for competition, health and safety, employment	Economic growth and the business cycle
	Unemployment rates and policies
Social factors	**Technological factors**
Education	Advances in technology
Customer demographics	Role of internet
Cultural issues	Spending on technology
Lifestyle issues/attitude to work	
Tastes and fashion	

Table 3.1: What to consider when doing a PEST analysis

PROJECT PROMPT

Remember that you only have to carry out a small-scale project. Not every factor is relevant or important for every situation. If you chose to construct a PEST or SWOT analysis for your project, only include factors that apply to you. For example, social factors are likely to be most important for an enterprise selling products to consumers. For school-based projects, school rules may replace laws and political stability or tax guidelines are unlikely to be relevant.

You could use the templates at the end of this chapter to help you with your PEST and SWOT analyses.

SWOT analysis

A SWOT analysis identifies current internal strengths and weaknesses and potential external opportunities and threats for an individual idea or project. Relevant issues are listed in Table 3.2.

Chapter 3: Opportunities, risk, legal and ethical considerations

Strengths	Weaknesses
• Internal features that the enterprise is good at and can be controlled • Factors may include: develops new products, good reputation, good location	• Internal features that the enterprise has control over which need to be improved • Factors may include: lack of cash flow, low production capacity, poor quality products
Opportunities	**Threats**
• External changes that the enterprise cannot control which they could benefit from • Factors may include: economic growth in the economy, population increase	• External changes or events that cannot be controlled which could place the enterprise or project at risk • Factors may include: increase in competition, changes in legal controls

Table 3.2: What to consider when doing a SWOT analysis

Internal factors include products, prices, costs, profit, performance, quality, people, skills, reputation and processes.

External factors include markets, fashion, seasonality, trends, competition, economics, population, politics, society, culture, technology, the environment, and the media.

Each factor can be seen as a positive or negative issue. Leadership could be either a strength or weakness. Developments in technology may mean the decrease in demand for an existing product, but at the same time creates an opportunity to offer a new product that could be more successful.

ACTIVITY 3.2

Carry out a simple SWOT analysis of your school. For example, what does your school do that means people would prefer to go to it? Are there any changes in government policy that your school could take advantage of? What could your school do better at? Is there anything other schools are doing that make them popular?

You could use the template at the end of this chapter to help you with your SWOT analysis.

> **TIP**
>
> Things to remember when constructing a SWOT analysis:
> - Focus on key points and issues that are likely to be important.
> - Be honest in your assessment. Otherwise it could lead to making incorrect decisions later.
> - Identify strengths and weaknesses in relation to any potential competitors – what could give your enterprise an advantage or put you at a disadvantage?
> - Keep it brief – a SWOT analysis is designed to be a simple one-page document.

Step 2: Analyse the implications of each risk

For each risk identified, consider the following questions:

- What are the chances of it happening?
- What are the potential consequences for the project if it did happen?

Remember, each risk and its consequences can have positive or negative effects.

An entrepreneur tries to balance the potential negative effects against the potential rewards of its actions. If the possible rewards can outweigh the negative risks a project is likely to proceed.

MINI CASE STUDY

Andrew Mupuya, Uganda

Andrew was a 16-year-old student when he founded YELI, Uganda's first paper bag production company. He got the idea after the government introduced a new law stopping businesses from using plastic bags to help protect the environment.

To start his enterprise, Andrew worked out he would need 36 000 Ugandan shillings ($10). He had no savings so he raised $7 by selling 70 kilos of used plastic bottles and borrowed $3 from his schoolteacher. He used the internet to find out how to make paper bags. All bags are made by hand as Andrew cannot afford a machine.

Question:

Explain two possible risks Andrew's new enterprise might face

Chapter 3: Opportunities, risk, legal and ethical considerations

Step 3: Decide whether the risk is worth it

The entrepreneur is the only person who can answer this question and will be influenced by their attitude to risk.

Using the information gathered in Step 2, a decision has to be made about which risks are worth taking. At this point the entrepreneur may decide that one or more of the risks are too high and the idea or project should be stopped.

Step 4: Plan to manage the risk

Having decided to carry on with the project, the entrepreneur has to decide how to deal with each of the main risks.

Remember, you are looking to reduce the chances of negative risks but not lose the chance for potential rewards.

Think MATE!

Figure 3.3: Think MATE to help you manage risk

Strategies to do this include:

- **M**itigate: Try to reduce the risk by changing what you do.
- **A**ccept: If there is nothing you can do about a given risk, be prepared or set aside money in the budget for any negative effects of the risk happening.
- **T**ransfer: Let someone else take the risk. For example, pass responsibility for key tasks to someone outside the organisation so they manage it.
- **E**liminate: ... the hazard (don't do it). Remember that if you try to avoid a risk, you may also have to give up the positive opportunity.

PROJECT PROMPT

In your project you will need to identify two or three stages from your action plan that you think are likely to be the most important.

To help you work these out, think about what could happen if this stage did not go ahead as planned and how this would affect the rest of your project. Outline the steps or changes you could make to ensure that this stage went ahead as planned. If something did go wrong, what would be your back-up plan?

Reducing risk

There are many different ways to reduce risk, including:

- detailed research including market research, use of financial projections and cash flow forecasts, use of PEST and SWOT analysis
- asking for advice from formal and informal sources of help and support
- careful planning by producing a business plan or action plan
- spreading the risk (also known as diversification) by selling different products or selling to different markets.

ACTIVITY 3.3

You live five miles from school. You travel to school by bus. The bus leaves at 7.30 a.m. It takes 15 minutes to walk to the bus station. Your alarm goes off at 7.00 a.m. It is exam time, but you are worried that you will be late for school.

1 Write down what would happen if you did nothing.
2 Think of possible strategies you could use to reduce or avoid this problem.

Which option would you choose? Explain why you have chosen this option rather than any other.

Step 5: Monitor the risk

As risks (and opportunities) change over time it is important to review and reassess the risks and actions taken as you carry out your enterprise. Changes because of external or internal factors can alter the amount of risk associated with a given action. An enterprise will have to respond, possibly changing what it does, to ensure that the overall outcome is positive.

Attitudes to risk

Everyone has a different view of risk. Some people like taking risks while others will avoid them.

There are three main attitudes to risk:

1 Risk-averse: Someone who will attempt to avoid any possibility of risk.
2 Risk-keen: Someone who is willing to accept a level of risk.
3 Risk-reducer: Someone who will attempt to limit the likelihood and amount of possible risk.

Your attitude to risk will influence your decisions and actions. For example, an entrepreneur who is risk averse will manage risk in a different way to an entrepreneur who is risk keen.

Chapter 3: Opportunities, risk, legal and ethical considerations

MINI CASE STUDY

Andrew Mupuya, Uganda (continued)

Andrew has no machine. If he is risk-keen, he could just buy a machine and hope that he can sell enough paper bags to pay for it. If he is risk-averse, he would decide to carry on making them by all by hand. As a risk-reducer, he may investigate all the possible advantages and disadvantages and try to work out if it is a risk he is willing to take. For example, he could use data to work out possible costs and potential sales, and discuss the plan with employees and lenders before making a decision to buy a machine or not.

Question:

What would you do?

Remember there is no 'right' attitude. Attitudes can and do change depending on the situation.

ACTIVITY 3.4

This activity can be done as either an individual or as part of a group. You have 20 minutes. The goal is to build the tallest tower possible. The rules are as follows:

- You can only use paper and paper clips.
- The tower must be free-standing and able to support itself for 30 seconds before it is measured.
- You are not allowed to touch or interfere with anyone else's tower.

The person or team with the tallest tower wins. How much risk are you willing to take?

Legal obligations

Legal considerations feature in PEST analysis and represent external factors in SWOT analysis.

Governments introduce laws and regulations to provide protection for different stakeholders to stop them being exploited. These include:

- Employment: Employment contracts state the terms of the job and what to do if there are any problems. This can be used to prevent or resolve disagreements. Minimum wage laws guarantee all workers a basic amount for work done. Laws also exist to prevent workers being unfairly treated because of factors such as race, gender or physical disability.

- Production: Health and safety laws set minimum standards to ensure safe working conditions for all employees.
- Marketing and selling: An enterprise has to be careful about what they say about the product or service they are offering. Laws exist to protect customers against misleading promotions and faulty or dangerous products.
- Finance: From providing or offering finance to completing business deals there are many laws and guidelines to ensure the correct documents are used and stakeholder interests are protected.

Note: you will not be assessed on specific laws in the exam, but you must be able to explain how they could affect an enterprise and its stakeholder. For example, an increase in the minimum wage will mean employees should receive more pay. With more disposable income they can buy more goods and services that can help other businesses in the local community. Higher wage costs could lead to a lower profit, reducing the return for owners. The enterprise may try to pass on the extra cost in the form of higher prices. Some customers may not be able (or willing) to pay the higher price.

ACTIVITY 3.5

Explain the possible effects on stakeholders of each of the following:
- restrictions on the type of materials that can be used in food
- new laws restricting where products can be advertised.

Ethical considerations

When setting up and running an enterprise, an entrepreneur must consider the effect of its actions on others (in the community). The effect can be positive or negative.

ACTIVITY 3.6

A takeaway coffee shop uses resources and energy. The enterprise provides jobs and income to local people who can then buy products from other local enterprises. The organisation may also sometimes support community activities by providing sponsorship to sports or arts groups. However, it serves its coffee in free disposable cups which are often thrown away and may add to littering and pollution.

Does the coffee shop's use of disposable cups make it a bad company?

Chapter 3: Opportunities, risk, legal and ethical considerations

Many enterprises, including social enterprises and charities, will try to maximise the amount of positive social impact they can create.

> **KEY TERM**
>
> **Ethics:** Moral values and principles that govern a person's behaviour or the conducting of an activity.

Being **ethical** involves actions and behaviour that go beyond what is legally required. Some enterprises will choose to be ethical in how they operate. An ethical enterprise will consider the impact of its decisions on all its stakeholders, not just the owners.

Ethics and profit can conflict. Being ethical can lead to higher wage and inventory costs, which can lower profit.

For example:

- How much to pay its workers? Paying the minimum wage may not be a living wage.
- Should child labour be used? In many countries the use of child workers is seen as exploitation.
- Should Fair Trade products be used or sold? Such items are generally more expensive as they guarantee a fair price to the producers.
- Paying a fair price to suppliers might lower the enterprise's profits.
- What should the enterprise do with any profit made? Should it donate some of its profits to charities or good causes?

Being ethical has both advantages and disadvantages.

- An ethical brand image can lead to a better reputation, which can help attract customers.
- The enterprise may be seen as a good employer and so is able to attract and retain employees.
- Suppliers may be willing to offer better terms as they are receiving a fair price for their products.
- Lenders may be more willing to offer help and support.
- It could be difficult for the enterprise to source materials and products.
- The increased cost of purchasing raw materials can force the enterprise to charge higher prices.
- The enterprise could gain support from the Fair Trade movement.
- Being ethical can provide a unique selling point (USP) and so may be used as a promotional tool.

Exam-style questions

This scenario is inspired by a true story. Find out more at www.hijup.com

Diajeng saw an opportunity in Indonesia's large population of Muslim women. Diajeng felt she did not have a lot of choice when it came to work clothes. Having talked to a friend about her idea, she decided to start up an online website offering fashion clothing and accessories. Diajeng knew there were many risks – including finance and meeting laws. All marketing is done through social media. Being ethical is important to Diajeng.

1 Define 'opportunity'. [2]

2 Explain two ways in which changes in taste and fashion might create opportunities for Diajeng's enterprise. [4]

3 Explain how you dealt with two risks in your enterprise project. [6]

4 Explain **two** advantages to Diajeng's enterprise of being ethical. [6]

5 Her friend told Diajeng about the laws and regulations that could affect employment, marketing, production and selling. Discuss, using examples, how an enterprise could be affected by laws and regulations in **two** of these areas. [10]

TIP

Always read the question carefully to ensure you have the correct focus before attempting to answer it. Check whether it refers to your own enterprise or a case study.

Summary

You should know:

- an entrepreneur must be able to identify opportunities and risks involved in enterprise and decide what to do about each one
- the legal obligations and ethical considerations that an entrepreneur must be aware of.

Template 1: How to conduct a PEST analysis

Use these categories to identify external factors that could impact your enterprise project.

Political factors	Economic factors
Social factors	Technological factors

Template 2: How to conduct a SWOT analysis

It is usual for a business to have several strengths, weaknesses, opportunities and threats.

Here are some questions relating to strengths, weaknesses, opportunities and threats. You should try to think about and answer these when thinking about your enterprise project.

Strengths	Weaknesses
1 What advantages does your business have? 2 What do you do better than anyone else? 3 What unique resources do you have to use that no one else can use? 4 What do other people see as your key strengths? 5 What factors mean people prefer to use your business over other businesses? 6 What is the business USP (unique selling point)?	1 What can you improve? 2 What should you avoid doing? 3 What do other people see as the weakness in your business? 4 What factors mean people might choose to use your competitors over you?
Opportunities	**Threats**
1 What opportunities can you spot in the market? 2 Are there any interesting trends in the market that you can take advantage of? 3 Are there any changes in technology that you can take advantage of? 4 Are there any changes in government policy that you can take advantage of? 5 Are there any local events that you can take advantage of?	1 What obstacles do you face? 2 What are your competitors doing? 3 Are there any changes in technology that might cause you problems? 4 Are there any changes in government policy that might cause you problems? 5 Could changes in consumer tastes cause you problems?

Chapter 4
Market research

Learning summary

In this chapter you will learn about:

- methods of identifying potential customers
- the effectiveness of these methods for different enterprises.

Purpose of market research

A successful entrepreneur has to take customer needs into account when developing or selling a product or service. **Market research** provides information needed to help make informed decisions.

> **KEY TERM**
>
> **Market research:** The process of collecting, collating and analysing data about customers, competitors or a market.

Accurate market research provides information:

- to find out about customer needs and wants
- about the market and competitors
- to help reduce the risk of introducing or selling new products
- to help plan marketing communications
- to help make decisions such as which idea or option to select or reject
- to evaluate success.

This information helps ensure that the products offered are what customers are willing to buy and at what price. Knowing customer needs can help an enterprise to remain competitive as well as maintain loyalty and sales.

Methods of market research

Different types of information can be collected in different ways.

Quantitative data is numerical information usually obtained from sales figures, surveys and questionnaires and is easy to present in charts or tables. While qualitative data is information based on opinions and reasons obtained from using visits, interviews and focus groups. The results are more detailed but they can be difficult to represent in tables and charts, as it is hard to compare individual opinions.

Primary market research

Primary research (or field research) involves collecting original information. The enterprise can select both the questions and who is asked to ensure the information is clearly focused on what it wants to know.

> **KEY TERM**
>
> **Primary research (field research):** Collecting new information or data for a specific purpose.

Examples include:

- **Surveys and questionnaires** – asking people a list of set questions. They can be done on-line, face to face or sent out by post. This is a relatively cheap way to gain information as large numbers of people can be asked the same simple questions. More people can be asked which increases the sample size. This can help reduce the risk of bias. The questions must be carefully designed as poorly worded, misleading or the wrong questions can lead to the poor decisions being made. This could result in higher costs, wasted resources and lost revenue. It can take a long time to collect all the questionnaires and people may not complete the surveys.

- **Interviews** – interviewers ask individuals a number of questions. This method can provide more detailed answers, as there is time to explore the answers given to questions. Interviews tend to provide higher response rates than surveys. However, interviews take a long time to complete. Fewer people are asked which means the sample size is smaller than surveys. Like questionnaires, there is also a risk of interviewer bias.
- **Consumer panels and focus groups** – gathering together a selection of people who have similar characteristics to the target market to give their opinions on a product or service. This allows for highly detailed information from a selected group of customers. However, the sample size is very small and other group members can influence what others in the group say or do. Focus groups are expensive and time consuming to arrange.
- **Observations** – watching or recording what people do or buy. This can provide an insight into what people do, but you cannot ask questions about why or what they behave this way. This means the information gathered can be limited or misleading. This is a cheap method as all someone has to do is watch what happens for an agreed period of time and questions do not need to be prepared.
- **Test marketing** – introducing a new product to a small number of potential customers to see their reaction to it. An entrepreneur can see if the product could appeal to a wider market or whether it needs to be changed or withdrawn. This approach is expensive and takes time. It could also alert competitors to what you are doing. This could limit the potential competitive advantage of the new product.

Primary research can help an enterprise in a number of ways, including:

- surveys and questionnaires to identify what customers need or want
- interviews with customers or previous enterprises to find out a good place to sell
- observation of buying habits
- focus groups to find out customers views as a way to measure customer satisfaction.

ACTIVITY 4.1

On your own take a few minutes to consider the following questions:

Have you ever been asked to take part in market research? What was it for? What typed of questions were you asked? Which style of questions do you like?

Discuss your results with others in your class? What are the similarities and differences? You can use this information when carrying out market research.

Write down two possible questions you could ask if you use a questionnaire as part of your market research for your enterprise project.

Asha's market stall

Asha has a market stall selling key rings and stationery. She decides to carry out some market research to identify new products. The results show that there is a high demand for cell (mobile) phone cases.

Write down possible questions Asha could have asked if she used a questionnaire. For each one, explain why you think this is a suitable question for her to ask.

1   Identify two possible questions Asha could ask in her market research. [2]
2   Explain two methods of primary market research Asha could use. [6]
3   Explain two suitable methods of market research you could use for your enterprise project. [6]

Chapter 4: Market research

PROJECT PROMPT

There is no set length for a questionnaire. The important thing is to make sure the questions are suitable for what you want to know. Always try to test out questions before using them with potential customers. This allows you to check that the questions make sense, and will allow you to find out the information you want.

Secondary market research

Using existing sources of information can provide useful data about the market in general and trends.

Secondary research (or desk research) is much cheaper and quicker to collect than primary research.

> **KEY TERM**
>
> **Secondary research (desk research):** The use of information that already exists and was originally collected for a different purpose.

However, care is needed. The data, which has been collected for a different purpose, may not provide the specific information needed to identify potential customers. This is because the questions asked might not be relevant to your enterprise or idea, or the wrong people were questioned and the information may be out of date. Any of these issues could lead to the wrong decisions being taken.

Examples include:

- **Existing data from your sales records** – internal records such as past years sales can help indicate which products are popular. This information is free and easy to obtain. It can also be kept secret from your competitors. However, the data may be incomplete and, if it is a new project or enterprise, there may be no information available.
- **Newspaper and internet articles** – can provide a wealth of general information on markets or trading conditions and trends in the market.
- **Trade organisations and journals** – these can provide industry-specific data for its members
- **Government statistics** – including census records can provide information about population, income and economic data. Such information is usually free and can be useful to identify trends over time.
- **Company and market research reports** – these can be a good source of market and competitor information. You may have to pay to access the data and it may be incomplete.
- **Market research agencies** – these organisations carry out research for other people. They will often provide information to other enterprises or individuals for a fee.

Secondary data is useful to:
- show what products are in demand and who is buying them
- identify the number of competitors or their sales
- identify a gap in the market not being exploited
- illustrate which products are successful in other areas
- identify costs for the enterprise
- find target markets
- compare the adverts of competing enterprises to compare effectiveness or get ideas
- spot trends and help identify what may happen in future.

Effectiveness of different methods of market research

There is no best method. Each approach has its advantages and disadvantages.

There are three key factors to consider:

1. The **type of information.** Decide what you want to know about your customers, market or competitors. This will influence the research methods chosen. It is often necessary to use a combination of methods to identify all the information.
2. **Time available.** A simple research activity will not take as much time as a larger project. Different methods need different amounts of time to complete. How much time does the enterprise have to carry out the research and analyse the results?
3. **How much you are able to spend.** Successful and established enterprises are likely to have a larger research budget than new enterprises, including your enterprise project.

	Primary	Secondary
Advantages	Up-to-date information	Readily available
	Other enterprises have no access to the data	Low or no cost
	You can ask the specific questions you want answers to	Can provide lots of additional helpful information not previously considered
Disadvantages	Expensive to collect	May not be relevant for the selected purpose
	Takes time to collect	Can be out of date

Table 4.1: The advantages and disadvantages of primary and secondary research

Chapter 4: Market research

PROJECT PROMPT

You do not need to use lots of different methods of market research. A simple questionnaire can provide enough data for you to use as evidence for your project. Chose one or two appropriate methods to find out information you need. Spend time analysing the results and use the data as evidence to support your decisions.

You can use the template at the end of this chapter to help with your market research.

ACTIVITY 4.2

For each of the following scenarios, identify two or three possible methods of market research they might use. Give reasons for your choices.
- An entrepreneur plans to set up a garden tidy service, and wants to know if it is likely to be popular with potential customers.
- An established retailer plans to open ten new shops next year, and wants to find out the best locations to choose.

ACTIVITY 4.3

Oris is planning to set up a food stall. Look at the following questions:
- Do you think orange is a good flavour for a drink?
- How popular to you think this product will be with children and adults?
- Do you always eat breakfast?

How helpful do you think these questions are? Why? How could Oris have worded the questions differently?

TIP

Keep questions simple. Do not worry about asking another question to ensure you get the information you need.

Presenting results

It is important to display the results in a form that is easy to understand. The method chosen depends on what information is being presented and whom it is for.

There are many ways to present information, including:

Tables: A simple record of facts and figures presented in rows and columns. Tables can contain a lot of data but it is not easy to see trends quickly.

Sizes of bags	Number of businesses
Small	45
Medium	35
Large	20

Figure 4.1: Example of a table

Bar charts: A good way of seeing information quickly and easily. However, bar charts can only show a small number of simple figures, such as when there is a single variable like price or sales.

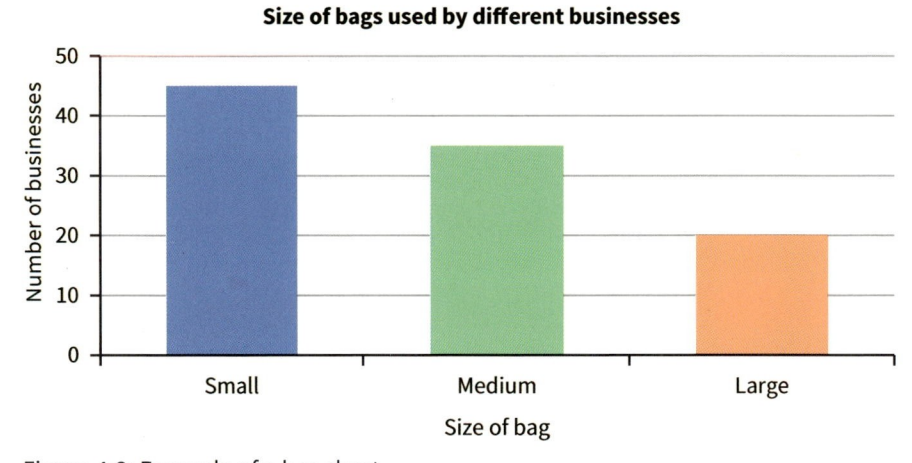

Figure 4.2: Example of a bar chart

Pie charts: Pie charts show you proportions. This is useful for simple comparisons between different options for the same question. It is easy to see results quickly but the values shown are percentages rather than actual totals.

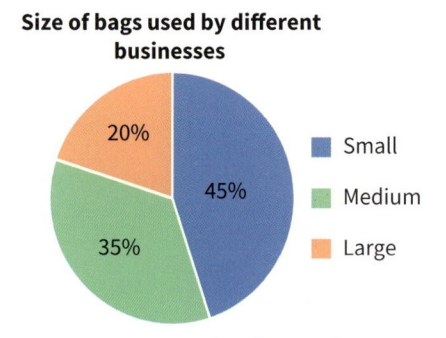

Figure 4.3: Example of a pie chart

Chapter 4: Market research

Graphs: Graphs can show you the relationship between two sets of numbers.

Number of bags used each year

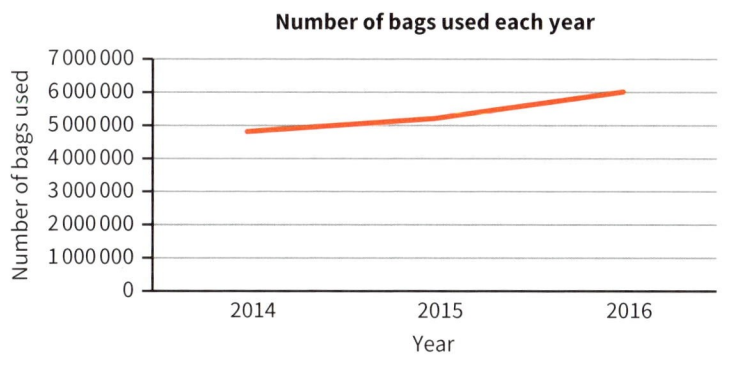

[Line graph showing Number of bags used on y-axis (0 to 7 000 000) against Year on x-axis (2014, 2015, 2016), with the line rising from approximately 4 800 000 in 2014 to 6 000 000 in 2016.]

Figure 4.4: Example of a line graph

There are other methods, including pictograms in which data is represented by symbols of the item being displayed. This is good for visual impact but difficult to represent exact numbers.

> **TIP**
>
> Always try to select a suitable way to present your data. Remember to label the chart and include a title explaining what it shows.

ACTIVITY 4.4

Oris started looking for a good location for his food stall. He carried out an observation looking at the number of people who visited a popular shopping centre one day.

Choose a suitable way or ways to present this information. Give reasons for your choice.

Time	Number of people walking past	Number of people eating food
1000 – 1529	45	15
1100 – 1129	60	30
1200 – 1259	120	90
1300 – 1359	80	60
1400 – 1459	75	60
1500 – 1559	60	40
1600 – 1659	80	60

Using market research data

It is important to carefully analyse all results. Let the results guide your decisions. Don't just select the information that confirms what you would like to do, and ignore other important data. If you do not have clear results, you might need to carry out more research.

> **ACTIVITY 4.5**
>
> Read the following analysis:
>
> I asked businesses what size bag they offered to customers. I asked this question because I wanted to know which type of bag was most popular. The results showed that 45 businesses used small bags, 32 used medium bags and 20 used large bags. Using this information I was able to decide which size bags to make.
>
> What is wrong with this analysis? Give reasons for your answer. How could it be improved?

Whichever method you use, always make clear reference to the results when using the information as evidence to support decisions made. Do not simply state the numbers or results. Always try to explain what the information means and how it helps to make decisions.

> **MINI CASE STUDY**
>
> ## Harry's handmade t-shirts
>
> For example:
>
> Harry loved designing things. He had the idea to sell his original hand-printed designs onto white t-shirts. His market research showed that 95 per cent of people liked his designs but 60 per cent of his customers would prefer coloured t-shirts.
>
> How does this information help Harry's enterprise?
>
> Harry could ignore this data, but it could reduce the number of potential customers by 60 per cent. It would be sensible for Harry to produce a range of colours. This means he may have to recruit more workers leading to an increase in costs and therefore a lower profit margin. However, by knowing his customer preferences at an early stage he has time to plan to overcome any potential problems.

Chapter 4: Market research

Exam-style questions

(Inspired by a true story. For more information visit www.LuvUrSkin.com.au)

Izzi couldn't use shop-made hand cream and lip balm. Her mother said she would have to use baby products or make her own. Izzi didn't want to use baby products, as she was eight, so she made her own. When her friends starting asking where they could buy the lip balm and other skin care products, Izzi wondered if she should start selling it. She decided to carry out some market research.

1 Define 'secondary market research'. [2]
2 Identify two possible advantages to Izzi's enterprise of using market research. [6]
3 Izzi carried out market research to identify potential customers. Discuss the two most suitable methods of research that she could have been used to identify potential customers. [10]
4 Evaluate the methods of market research that could have been suitable for your enterprise project to use to identify potential customers. [15]

Summary

You should know:

- there are many methods of market research that an enterprise can use to help identify potential customers
- each method has advantages and disadvantages, so selecting the right method is important
- results can be presented in different ways
- these results can be analysed to help make decisions.

Template 3: Conducting market research

1	Decide the information you want to find out (WHAT)	• Work out what you want to know before you start writing any questions. • Check to see if any of the data is already available. This can save you time from having to collect it.
2	Identify the potential target respondents (WHO)	• Who will you ask your questions to? The people you ask should represent your potential target market. Think about issues such as gender, age, interests and location.
3	Choose a suitable method(s) of research (HOW)	• After defining what and who to ask, decide on the method. The two methods you are most likely to use are questionnaires and/or interviews.

4	Develop the questions	• Questions should be clear and simple to understand. When writing questions, try to remember the following guidelines:
		  • Questions should be clearly worded and response options should be easy to complete.
		  • Avoid technical words and jargon.
		  • Don't ask leading questions (e.g. how unfair is it that the school doesn't let us use phones in class?).
		  • Don't try to ask too much in one question (e.g. do you think low prices and good quality is important when…?)
		  • Try to include a mixture of questions so that the respondent does not lose interest.
		  • If you want a single answer, choices need be unique and not overlap e.g. 10–20 and 20-30 could be changed to 10–19, 20–29.
		  • Allow for all possible options in answers. It may be helpful to include an 'Other, please specify' option.

5	Put questions in a logical order	• The first question(s) should be easy to answer, and make the respondent feel comfortable. • Each question should follow on from the previous one. • Group questions together by topic to help them flow better.
6	Make sure there are not too many questions	• Keep the questionnaire or interview short. People are more likely to lose interest if the research takes too long. • Remove any unnecessary questions.
7	Test questions before use	• It is a good idea to ask a few people outside of your group to check that the questions make sense and will collect the information you want. • Make any changes before carrying out the research.
8	Carrying out the market research	• Make sure to ask the correct respondents (as identified in Step 2). • Think about how you present yourself to the respondent. Be friendly and interested in what they have to say. • Try to avoid bias in how you ask each question, as you do not want to act in a way that may influence what people say. • Always finish by thanking people for their time.

62

Chapter 5
Business planning

Learning summary

In this chapter you will learn about:

- the different aims and objectives of different enterprises
- how aims influence the activities of enterprises
- the purpose and importance of action plans
- contents of action plans
- methods of monitoring and the importance of updating action plans
- the purpose, importance and contents of business plans
- methods of monitoring business plans and reasons for updating business plans.

Business objectives

Why? We all have a reason for doing something. Most enterprises have an overall goal or idea about what it would like to achieve in the future. To achieve it requires planning.

> **KEY TERMS**
>
> **Aim:** An overall goal that an enterprise wants to achieve.
>
> **Objective:** A specific target that an enterprise wants to reach so it can achieve its aims.

This involves breaking the goal down into smaller steps that can be reviewed to monitor its progress towards achieving the goal.

The main difference between an **aim** and **objective** is time.

Aims are long-term and objectives are short-term. Aims are general statements of intent. Objectives are specific targets set to help achieve its overall aim.

For example, an enterprise may aim to increase profits in a fair way. To do this, the objective is to increase profits by three per cent by the end of the year.

Objectives should be specific, measurable, achievable, realistic and time-based (or SMART).

Setting objectives provides a focus and a sense of direction. This can help motivate employees as they know what they are working towards. It also acts as a measure against which progress can be monitored. Plans can then be made about how to achieve these targets.

Objectives may include:

- **Survival** – try to keep the enterprise running
- **Maximising profit** – try to make as much profit as possible
- **Satisfying profit** – try to make enough profit to keep the owners comfortable
- **Growth** – try to increase its size including market share
- **Sales growth** – try to make as many sales as possible
- **Sales revenue** – try to make as much revenue as possible
- **Cash flow** – try to ensure they have enough cash to pay its day-to-day costs
- **Provide a good service** – try to provide a positive experience to its customers
- **Environmental** – try to protect the environment
- **Ethical** – try to treat all its stakeholders fairly
- **Social** – try to meet the needs of less fortunate members of society
- **Not-for-profit** – try to use any surplus revenue to help it achieve its purpose or mission.
- **Legal compliance** – meet all laws and regulations to avoid legal action or damage to reputation

Chapter 5: Business planning

Not all enterprises are interested in maximising profit or growth. Some enterprises are guided by the values or principles that are important to them. These can be social, service-based, ethical or environmental.

Objectives can and do change over time. Once an objective is achieved a new target is needed. Changes in the external environment – e.g. a new competitor, developments in technology and different economic conditions – can influence the objectives set.

ACTIVITY 5.1

Investigate two or three enterprises, ideally small local ones. What are their aims and objectives? How do the aims and objectives of each enterprise vary? Can you think of possible reasons for this?

How aims influence the activities of enterprises

The overall goals of an enterprise will determine its actions. Different enterprises have different aims and objectives. An entrepreneur will take decisions to help achieve their chosen objectives. To increase profit they may look for ways to increase sales and decrease costs. This could mean increasing prices and lowering the number of employees. To expand, the entrepreneur may open more shops or try to buy a rival enterprise.

Other organisations, such as social enterprises and charities, are more interested in providing a service (see Chapter 1). They may look for ways to increase the number of people they help. Keeping prices and costs low will be important so more people can be helped.

Planning is important to help achieve aims and objectives. It allows an enterprise to use its resources and time effectively and help prepare for unexpected events. Planning can be short-term, medium-term or long-term.

An enterprise will use different planning tools, including action plans, business plans and marketing plans, as well as plans for negotiations and meetings.

Action plans

Poor planning is one reason why many enterprises fail. Planning helps make sure the right things are done at the right times.

An **action plan** provides a step-by-step framework of individual activities needed

KEY TERM

Action plan: A list of tasks that need to be completed in order for a set goal to be achieved.

to complete a project. It shows what needs to be done, when it needs to be done, by whom it needs to be done and how progress will be monitored.

> **PROJECT PROMPT**
>
> You must prepare an action plan as part of your project. The length and level of detail included will depend entirely on the size and type of project selected. If you are working as part of a group, you should have a larger-scale project so everyone has a chance to play a meaningful role in it. As such the action plan is likely to involve many more stages. The important thing to remember is that the action plan should be suitable for the scale of project, and detailed enough to help you set up, run and monitor what you need to do.

Purpose and importance of action plans

An action plan can help an entrepreneur:

- better understand what needs to be done so the right things are done at the right time

> **KEY TERM**
>
> **Prepare:** Present information in a suitable format.

- identify the key stages of a project by having to think carefully about what they want to do – this can stop them from doing the wrong things, which wastes time and effort
- identify potential obstacles and issues that need to be resolved so they can think about how to manage or avoid them
- keep track of who is responsible for what and when
- by acting as a checklist to monitor progress so that everything is done on time. Any problems or delays can then be spotted quickly and suitable steps can be taken before it's too late.

Format of an action plan

Task	Person responsible	Completion date	How progress will be monitored	Updates/ changes made

For your project, you need to identify which are the key activities (see Chapter 3).

You do not have to include this in your action plan – but it is helpful to keep a record any changes made, and why.

Figure 5.1: An example of an action plan

Chapter 5: Business planning

> **PROJECT PROMPT**
>
> You should prepare an action plan **before** you start the project. This will allow you to identify any problems and see how you will manage each one.
>
> **You can use the template at the end of this chapter to help create the action plan.**
>
> Your project action plan will not be assessed, but you will still be required to include it for reference and as evidence of your work.
>
> For your project the number of activities (stages) and level of detail will depend on the project chosen. A group project should be a bigger project so would include more activities so that everyone has the chance to have a meaningful role. If you work as part of a group you may agree an action plan together.

Stages in constructing an action plan

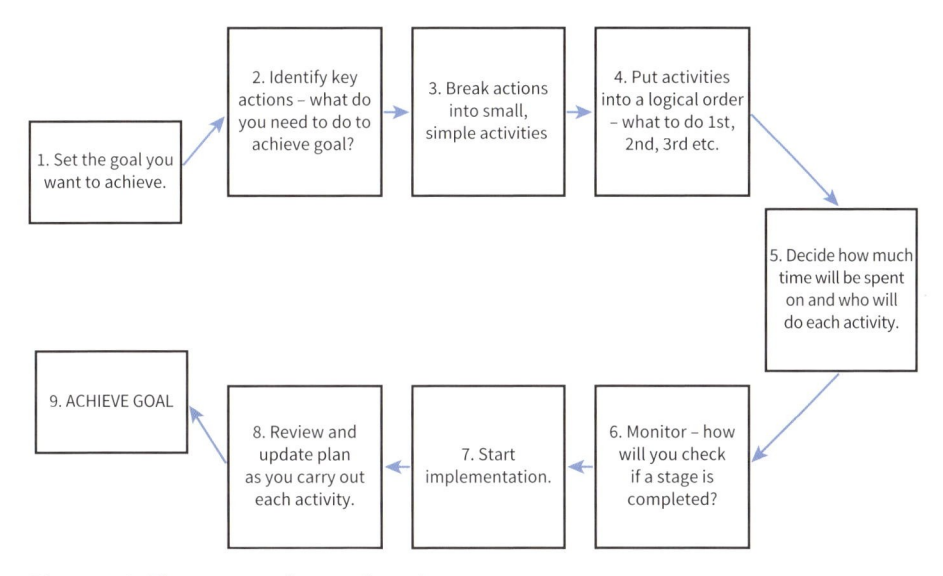

1. Set the goal you want to achieve.
2. Identify key actions – what do you need to do to achieve goal?
3. Break actions into small, simple activities
4. Put activities into a logical order – what to do 1st, 2nd, 3rd etc.
5. Decide how much time will be spent on and who will do each activity.
6. Monitor – how will you check if a stage is completed?
7. Start implementation.
8. Review and update plan as you carry out each activity.
9. ACHIEVE GOAL

Figure 5.2: The stages of an action plan

> **TIP**
>
> A good idea is to write each action on a separate piece of paper. This will make it easier to order them later.

Activities and timescales can and do change. So be prepared to adapt what you do.

> **PROJECT PROMPT**
>
> Do not worry if some activities change as you carry out the project. This is normal. Keep a note of any changes made, why each one was necessary and the effect of these changes for your project. You can use this information as evidence of your planning and implementation.

> **ACTIVITY 5.2**
>
> Imagine you have been asked to organise a food stall for a celebration or festival which is happening in a few weeks' time.
> Write a simple action plan that you could use to help you achieve your goal.

Planning to manage potential problems and issues

Some activities will be more important than others. A significant activity is one that would have a major negative impact on the project if it went wrong or didn't happen on time.

> **ACTIVITY 5.3**
>
> Olivia makes jam in her spare time, which she sells to friends and family. One of Olivia's friends has asked her to take part in a food festival in two weeks' time. For this, Olivia would need to produce 150 jars of jam. Olivia knows it will be difficult to complete the order so she has prepared an action plan. She has identified two significant activities – she only has one cooking pan to make jam, which is not large enough; and buying enough fruit may be a problem as it is near the end of the fruit season. She will also need to buy 150 glass jars and design the labels for the jars.
>
> Olivia has one pan so can only make 75 jars in the time available. Without another pan, she cannot meet the order. To overcome this, she could ask friends if she could borrow a pan. This would save money but there is no guarantee the pan would be suitable. Alternatively she could buy another pan. However, this would be expensive and she does not have the necessary finance, as she also needs to buy the jars and stickers so the jam can be sold. She thinks the best option would be ask the kitchen manager at school. She has been told the kitchen has

Chapter 5: Business planning

the right pan. She would have to plan for the negotiation. The preparation for this would take time but she is confident she can achieve a favourable outcome. Suggest ways in which Olivia could try to manage her fruit problem.

PROJECT PROMPT

For your project, you will need to identify two or three significant activities from your action plan. For each activity identify potential problems or issues and describe how you would try to manage each problem or issue. Think about why it is important that these activities happen when planned. Then write down the steps you could take to ensure that the activity does take place when necessary. Think about different options and explain why you have chosen the action you intend to use.

Methods of monitoring action plans

An action plan is a step-by-step guide to help you achieve your goal. However you also need to know if you are on track. **Monitoring** is simply how you **plan to check** whether a task has been completed or not.

KEY TERM

Monitor: To check or review the progress of something over a period of time.

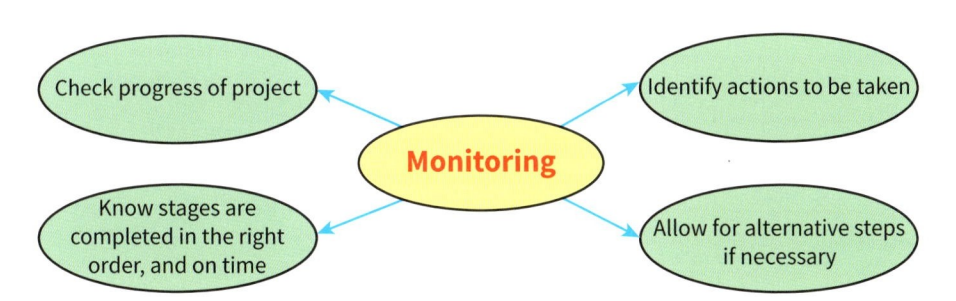

Figure 5.3: Why monitoring is important to an enterprise project

[Monitoring diagram with four connected nodes: Check progress of project; Identify actions to be taken; Know stages are completed in the right order, and on time; Allow for alternative steps if necessary]

A wide range of methods can be used for monitoring. For example:

- checklists (e.g. shopping lists, to-do lists)
- data (e.g. sales numbers, forecast or budgets, production numbers)

- measuring customer needs or customer satisfaction through surveys and interviews
- testing to check that a product is fit for purpose, or that equipment works
- reporting (e.g. provide updates at meetings).

Different activities will require different monitoring methods. Selecting a suitable one is important if it is to be effective. Keep the following in mind when choosing a monitoring method.

- What is its purpose – what do you need to check?
- Is it simple to use?
- Does it provide the information you require?

> **PROJECT PROMPT**
>
> In the monitoring section, do not simply describe the actions involved to complete the activity. This is not monitoring. Think about how you plan to check to see if it has been completed. It can be something simple, for example when purchasing materials you may use a shopping list to check items against it. This is fine, as the method selected is suitable for the activity.

The importance of updating action plans

Any plan is only a guide. Circumstances can and do change. For example, you might not be able to obtain the necessary permission to carry out your enterprise, or supplies you need might be unavailable.

If an action plan is to be helpful, you must check and review what is happening on a regular basis. This allows you to be aware of problems as soon as possible and adapt accordingly.

Business plans

A **business plan** is important for any enterprise, whether it is starting up or aiming to expand. It describes what the enterprise is going to do. Preparing a business plan makes the entrepreneur think carefully

> **KEY TERM**
>
> **Business plan:** A formal document that gives the aims of the enterprise and outlines ways those aims will be achieved.

about the aims of the business, the market and competition, its financial needs and resources. This can help to reduce risk.

The purpose and importance of a business plan

A business plan is used for many reasons:

- Acts as a focus so the entrepreneur thinks about what they are doing and why it is a good idea.
- Provides information about the market, competitors and the potential demand. This can help with marketing decisions.
- Identifies costs and financial needs. This can help the enterprise to arrange finance in advance and avoid potential cash flow problems.
- Provides evidence to show an idea is possible. This can be used to persuade others to offer credit or finance. Lenders will want to know they will be repaid.
- Makes the entrepreneur think ahead. This may help them to identify and avoid risks, or put in place measures to reduce them.
- It can be used to produce targets which the enterprise can use to measure success.
- Helps with organisation (e.g. decide structure, allocate job roles).

Contents of a business plan

- **Preliminary information:** e.g. details about the business including name and address, objectives, organisational structure and a simple description of the proposed idea
- **Marketing:** e.g. size of market, competition, pricing, promotion, product and place
- **Operations (production):** how the enterprise will work e.g. production details, resources
- **Human resources:** e.g. number of employees and who will have which roles
- **Financial:** e.g. key targets, cash flow forecast, break-even, budgets, income statement, balance sheet, sales revenue, costs.

MINI CASE STUDY

Business plan for Suki's Noodle Bar

Name of business	Suki's Noodle Bar
Type of organisation	Sole trader – Suki
Summary of idea	To set up a mobile noodle bar for use at the beach or local park depending on events and festivals being held
Business aim and objectives	To provide high quality noodles and healthy drinks to people at affordable prices To break-even within 6 months
Marketing:	
Product	High quality noodles and home made healthy drinks
Target market	Young people and families
Market research	Questionnaires carried out in local area, observations, Secondary research based on census See appendix for results
Price	Average price $2 for noodles and $1 for drinks
Place	Stall will be set up at various locations across the city
Promotion	Leaflets and social media Free samples will also be on offer at the stall
Operations	Stall with high quality cooking equipment on site (the equipment will cost $500 to buy). Materials to be obtained from local suppliers on a daily basis
Human resources	One full-time and one occasional helper: Suki – 2 years' experience as a chef One helper – volunteer (to be recruited as needed) Suki will be responsible for all activities. A helper will be available at busy times to prepare ingredients as needed.
Finance	In Year 1, total revenue is forecast to be $1 000 with total costs of $800 resulting in a profit of $200 in Year 1. See appendix for financial data

Chapter 5: Business planning

Question:

Suki has asked for a bank loan to buy equipment for her new enterprise.

Explain how the bank manager might use the following information when deciding whether to provide Suki a loan:

- Market research results
- Suki's previous experience

PROJECT PROMPT

You do not have to submit a business plan for your enterprise project. Some of the information found in a business plan is assessed but this is covered in your market research, financial data and marketing communication work.

A business plan may be used as evidence to support your negotiation section. If so, you could include it as supporting evidence.

Methods of monitoring business plans

Comparing actual numbers against those identified in budgets and marketing plan is an important way to check progress. An enterprise will consider a range of information depending on the objectives set.

Data could include:

- Financial data: Cash flow, profit, costs, sales numbers and revenue
- Operations data: Total level of output, output per employee
- Marketing data: Feedback from customer surveys, customer retention numbers, market share, number of people seeing your marketing communication
- Human resources data: Number of employees, attendance levels, hours worked.

Reasons for updating business plans

A business plan is a working document that can be used as a guide and to monitor progress. Plans cannot be completely accurate as they are based on historical information, projections and estimates about what is expected to happen. Internal and external factors change. For example:

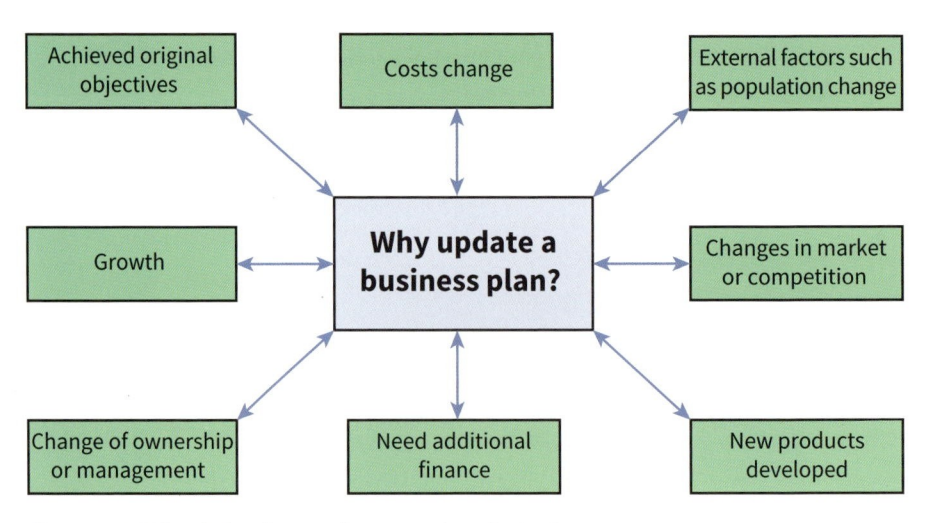

```
                    ┌──────────────────┐
┌──────────────┐    │   Costs change   │    ┌──────────────────────┐
│   Achieved   │    └──────────────────┘    │   External factors   │
│   original   │                            │   such as population │
│  objectives  │                            │       change         │
└──────────────┘                            └──────────────────────┘

┌──────────────┐    ┌──────────────────┐    ┌──────────────────────┐
│    Growth    │ →  │  Why update a    │ ←  │  Changes in market   │
│              │    │  business plan?  │    │    or competition    │
└──────────────┘    └──────────────────┘    └──────────────────────┘

┌──────────────┐    ┌──────────────────┐    ┌──────────────────────┐
│   Change of  │    │  Need additional │    │    New products      │
│  ownership   │    │      finance     │    │     developed        │
│or management │    └──────────────────┘    └──────────────────────┘
└──────────────┘
```

Figure 5.4: Why do business plans need updating?

If the business plan is not reviewed and updated to reflect such changes, wrong decisions may be taken, wasting time and money. For example, if demand falls you will need to reduce output, to avoid making unwanted products resulting in additional costs.

Chapter 5: Business planning

Exam-style questions

As a student Carlos had a part-time job cleaning people's houses. When he left school he decided to set up Carlos Cleaning (CC). He bought himself a bucket, some brushes and a bicycle to travel between jobs. His customers were very pleased with his work, and started recommending CC to their friends. One of his customers asked if he would like to clean their work office as well. Carlos was excited by this and knew of lots of friends who would be happy to work for CC. However, Carlos realised he would need to buy more equipment to complete all the work. He started to prepare his business plan before he went to ask for a bank loan.

1. Define 'action plan'. [2]
2. Explain two possible objectives that CC might have. [4]
3. Explain **two** reasons why a business plan might need to be updated. [4]
4. Evaluate how important a business plan was to CC. [10]
5. Good planning is necessary for any enterprise. Using examples, evaluate the importance of planning to the success of your enterprise project. [15]

Summary

You should know:

- the different aims and objectives for different types of enterprises
- how aims influence the activities of enterprises
- how identifying short term and long term goals can help an entrepreneur to decide on appropriate courses of action
- the purpose and importance of action plans and business plans
- action plans and business plans need to be reviewed and updated regularly.

Template 4: Action planning checklist

You will be expected to create an action plan when planning your enterprise project.

Here are some simple guidelines to help you.

Identify actions
• Can you list of all the possible activities that need to be done to achieve your goal? • Are there any activities that can be removed? • Which activities do you think might be significant – i.e. if they are delayed, could it affect the rest of the project? (Keep a note of these for later.) • Which activity should be done first, second etc.? (Try to put all activities into a logical order.)
Organise the activities
• How long is needed to complete each activity? • Are there any deadlines for certain activities that you need to be aware of and plan for? • Who will be responsible for each activity? • How will the progress of each activity be monitored? • What are the potential problems that need to be managed? (Hint: think about the significant activities.) • Have you decided on suitable actions to manage each identified problem? • Have you recorded all the information in a suitable format? (See the following table for an example of format you might use.)
Implement the plan
• Do you have a copy of the action plan with you as each activity is carried out? • Have you updated your plan as you go along? • Have you reviewed the plan to check that it is still on schedule? • Was each activity completed on time and as planned? If not, do you need to change the plan? If so, how? • How do these changes affect other activities or timings?

Chapter 5: Business planning

Use the following table to organise your activities for your enterprise project.

	Activity	Person responsible	Start date/ timings	Completion date	Monitoring
1	Loan	Deniz	asap	asap	to get the loan
2	Finding products	Sofi/David	now sep. 26	end of January	ongoing
3	Overseeing form	David	now	sep. 30	ongoing
4	analyzing results of form	Deniz	~~oct sep.~~ 2	~~oct sep.~~ 5	ongoing
5	ordering product	Sofi	Jan. 20	Jan 30	ongoing
6	place	David	now	Feb. 15	ongoing
7	price	All	Feb 20	Feb 22	ongoing
8					
9					
10					
11					
12					
13					
14					
15					

The number of activities will vary depending on each individual project.

Learning summary

In this chapter you will learn about:

- sources of finance including their advantages and disadvantages
- appropriate sources of finance for different situations.

Chapter 6: Sources of finance

Sources of finance

Enterprises need money for a variety of reasons. When a business is starting up it may need money to buy or rent premises, or to purchase equipment. As a business develops it may require additional funds for activities, such as introducing a new product or service, or replacing old and inefficient equipment.

There are many ways in which an enterprise can get the money that it needs; these are called **sources of finance**. It is important that enterprises use the right sources of finance for the situation they are in so that they do not end up with financial difficulties. For this reason many enterprises thoroughly research possible sources of finance, weighing up the advantages and disadvantages of each source to see which is the most suitable for their particular situation.

> **KEY TERMS**
>
> **Source of finance:** The way in which an enterprise gets the money it needs to finance an activity.
>
> **Finance:** The activities of an enterprise relating to money.
>
> **Start-up:** The period of an enterprise when it is first set up.
>
> **Internal sources of finance:** money that is found within the enterprise.
>
> **Interest:** Often, when an enterprise borrows money from a lender they will have to pay back the amount they borrow plus an agreed amount. The additional amount is known as the interest.

PROJECT PROMPT

As part of your project you will be expected to research potential sources of finance, weigh up the advantages and disadvantages of each, and decide which ones are most suitable for starting up your enterprise.

You can use the template at the end of this chapter to help research sources of finance.

Sources of finance suitable for start-up enterprises

Table 6.1 summarises the main types of **finance** that **start-up** enterprises can access.

Name of finance	Description	Advantages	Disadvantages
Personal savings (**internal source of finance**)	A small investment in a business, normally paid back with **interest** (a return on the investment).	You do not need approval to use your own money. If successful you get your money back plus interest.	If the enterprise is unsuccessful you may lose all the money you invested – this may cause hardship.

Table 6.1: Sources of finance available to start-ups

Name of finance	Description	Advantages	Disadvantages
Investment from family and friends (**external source of finance**)	A small investment in a business normally paid back with interest (a return on investment).	Family and friends will often be keen to support you and your enterprise. Usually charge lower interest than other lenders, such as banks.	If the enterprise is unsuccessful you may lose all the money that friends and family have invested – can cause upset as well as hardship.
Bank overdrafts (external source of finance)	A form of short term lending by the bank when there is no money left in the enterprise's bank account.	Can cover a short term financial issue.	A very short term option as interest is charged at a very high rate.
Bank/building society loan (external source of finance)	A larger, longer term investment paid back at an agreed interest rate.	Larger sums of money are available.	You need to provide detailed financial information to get the loan approved. Interest rates can be high. If you fail to make payments on the loan the bank may seize **assets** of the enterprise.
Leasing (external source of finance)	You rent a piece of equipment for a monthly fee but the equipment belongs to the leasing company.	Short term this is often cheaper than buying equipment outright. After a fixed time period the equipment is often updated to the latest model.	Long term this can be expensive because the fees may come to more than the equipment would have cost.

Table 6.1 (*Continued*)

Chapter 6: Sources of finance

Name of finance	Description	Advantages	Disadvantages
Mortgages (external source of finance)	A larger, longer term loan used to buy property and paid back at an agreed interest.	Large sums of money can be borrowed to buy property for the business. Generally a much lower rate of interest than other forms of borrowing.	You need to provide detailed financial information to get the mortgage approved. If you fail to make payments on the loan the bank may seize property that was bought using the mortgage.
Community sources (external source of finance)	Some community organisations set up funds that can be used for projects that support the community.	Can bring money into the community which improves the lives of those in the community. It does not have to be paid back.	You can only spend the money on a community project. If you do not use the money as agreed, it may be taken back from you.
Grants (external source of finance)	Money offered to enterprises, usually by governments, for specific projects.	Can bring income into enterprises for expensive projects. It does not have to paid back.	You can only spend the money on a specific project. If you do not use the money as agreed, it can be taken back from you.
Subsidies (external source of finance)	A government will sometimes provide a subsidy to a particular type of enterprise to support its development or for public benefit. The subsidy may be some form of cash payment or a reduced rate of tax.	Will either bring cash into the enterprise, or reduce the tax bill.	Only available for specific types of enterprise. The enterprise may have to meet certain conditions in order to get the subsidy.

Table 6.1 (*Continued*)

Name of finance	Description	Advantages	Disadvantages
Crowdfunding (external source of finance)	Using websites and social media to encourage large numbers of people to invest small amounts of money in return for a stake in the company, or other reward.	Although each person only invests a very small amount, those investments put together can raise a large sum for an enterprise.	If the enterprise fails then each investor loses their money. Some crowdfunding ventures never raise the money they want because they are poor at using the websites and social media.
Selling shares (external source of finance)	People invest money into your enterprise for a share of the ownership and the profits (called a dividend when paid to shareholders).	It is possible to raise a large amount of money by selling shares in an enterprise.	Shareholders expect to have their say in how the enterprise is run. Selling too many shares can open your enterprise up to being bought completely and taken over.

Table 6.1 (*Continued*)

MINI CASE STUDY

The Samphire Festival, UK

Samphire is an independent music and arts festival.

Founders Flora Blathwayt and Josh Beauchamp did not have the money to set up the festival but were confident that there were enough people interested in this type of event they chose to use crowdfunding via social media to get people to invest in their idea. For a small investment people would get something at the festival named after them, bigger investors would get discounted tickets and the largest investors could put their company name and logo on the main stage throughout the festival.

Founders of the Samphire Festival, Flora Blathwayt and Josh Beauchamp

So many people were interested that it broke crowdfunding records, gaining all the funding that it needed in a matter of days.

Chapter 6: Sources of finance

> **KEY TERMS**
>
> **External sources of finance:** Money that is found outside the enterprise.
> **Assets:** Objects that are owned by the business.
> **Founders:** The people who start a company.

Sources of finance for continuing trading and expansion

Table 6.2 summarises the main types of finance that an enterprise may access to continue trading or expand.

Name of finance	Description	Advantages	Disadvantages
Personal savings (internal source)	A small investment in a business normally paid back with interest (a return on the investment).	You do not need approval to use your own money. No interest paid.	If the enterprise is unsuccessful you may lose all the money you invested.
Retained profits	Money that is kept aside from the profits of the enterprise to be reinvested when it is needed.	You do not need approval to use this money and can use it as needed in the enterprise. You do not have to pay interest on this money.	If your enterprise has shareholders you may need to consult them regarding how much money you can retain because it will reduce the dividend they get paid. If your enterprise has shareholders they may impose conditions on how retained profits can be used.

Table 6.2: Sources of finance available to expand or continue trading

Name of finance	Description	Advantages	Disadvantages
Private institutions	Typically, a microfinance lender which aids people who do not have enough income to access traditional bank loans. Microfinance organisations focus on helping entrepreneurs succeed and as part of the loan agreement they require the borrower to take a money management course.	People with very little income can access small loans to help get them started as entrepreneurs. Borrowers get training on how to manage their money.	Interest is paid on the loan, often at a much higher rate than that which the traditional banks charge.
Venture capital	An individual or small group (venture capitalists) weigh up the risks and rewards of investing in an enterprise. If they invest they expect a share of the enterprise.	Most venture capitalists are experienced entrepreneurs with a lot of knowledge and skills that can help the enterprise. This can raise a lot of money for the enterprise.	Venture capitalists will expect to control a lot of decision-making within the enterprise to protect their investment. This can lead to conflict between the venture capitalist and the enterprise founders.

Table 6.2 (*Continued*)

Chapter 6: Sources of finance

Name of finance	Description	Advantages	Disadvantages
Issue shares	Offering additional shares in the enterprise to existing shareholders or new people. They invest money into the enterprise for a share of the ownership and profits (a dividend when paid to shareholders).	It is possible to raise a large amount of money by selling shares in an enterprise.	Shareholders may expect dividends. Selling too many shares can risk the enterprise being bought completely and taken over.

Table 6.2 (*Continued*)

ACTIVITY 6.1

Here are some sources of finance (in pink) and their definitions (in yellow). Write out the sources of finance with their correct definitions.

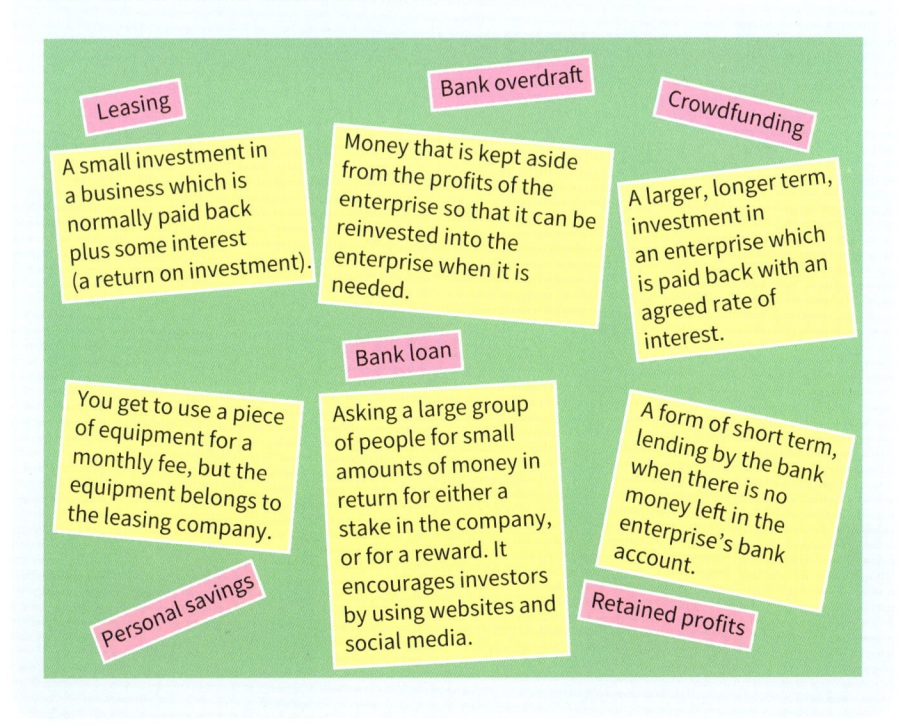

Leasing
A small investment in a business which is normally paid back plus some interest (a return on investment).

Bank overdraft
Money that is kept aside from the profits of the enterprise so that it can be reinvested into the enterprise when it is needed.

Crowdfunding
A larger, longer term, investment in an enterprise which is paid back with an agreed rate of interest.

Bank loan
You get to use a piece of equipment for a monthly fee, but the equipment belongs to the leasing company.

Asking a large group of people for small amounts of money in return for either a stake in the company, or for a reward. It encourages investors by using websites and social media.

A form of short term, lending by the bank when there is no money left in the enterprise's bank account.

Personal savings

Retained profits

Exam-style questions

1. Define the term 'retained profit'. [2]
2. Using the case study on the Samphire Festival, describe the source of funding used in this start-up enterprise. [2]
3. Describe, giving one advantage and one disadvantage, a potential source of finance for continued trading of the Samphire Festival. [4]
4. Referring to your enterprise project, discuss why you chose your source(s) of finance and evaluate if you made the correct choice for your enterprise. [10]
5. Manisha owns a successful t-shirt printing enterprise. She needs to buy a new printing machine to allow her to increase production. Discuss the advantages and disadvantages to Manisha of using a bank loan rather than other sources of finance. [10]

Summary

You should know:

- the advantages and disadvantages of different types of start-up funding
- the different types of funding for continuing trade and expansion.

Chapter 6: Sources of finance

Template 5: Choosing sources of finance

Item and cost of materials/ equipment	Source of finance	Advantage of source	Disadvantage of source	Choice of finance and reasons

Chapter 7
The concept of trade credit

Learning summary

In this chapter you will learn about:

- trade credit
- the advantage and disadvantage of trade credit to entrepreneurs, suppliers and customers.

Chapter 7: The concept of trade credit

Introduction

Sometimes an enterprise will not have the money to buy the things that it needs from its **suppliers**, but if they don't buy these things they might not be able to continue operating. In these situations some suppliers might let the enterprise have the things it needs on a buy-now, pay-later basis. This is called trade credit.

Trade credit between enterprises and their suppliers (trade payables)

> **KEY TERMS**
>
> **Supplier:** A person or organisation that provides the goods/materials or services that an enterprise needs in order to operate.
>
> **Trade payable:** the amount of money owed by the enterprise to suppliers, such as for raw material received but not paid for.
>
> **Revenue:** The money that comes into an enterprise from selling goods and services. To work out revenue you do a simple calculation: selling price x quantity sold = revenue.

Trade credit means that an enterprise can buy the items that it needs and then have an agreed number of days in which to pay the supplier. Money owed by the enterprise to its suppliers for items bought on credit is known as **trade payables**. This means the enterprise can make its product, sell it, and pay the bill with the **revenue** that it brings in. Or, if the enterprise already has the money to pay the bill, it can be kept in the enterprise's bank account longer and gain more interest.

If the enterprise pays within the agreed number of days then it only pays what was agreed. However, if they go over the agreed number of days there will be penalties, such as a percentage increase in the bill. Some agreements also have rewards for early repayments, such as a percentage discount on the agreed price.

Example: A simple trade agreement.

Trade credit agreement: 30 days.

If you pay your bill within 10 days you will get a 5% discount on the total bill.

If you do not pay your bill within 30 days you will be charged a penalty as shown:

30 to 60 days	An additional 5% on the original bill.
60 to 90 days	An additional 10% on the original bill
90 days or more	An additional 20% on the original bill

A start-up enterprise is unlikely to get trade credit with their suppliers. This is because they have not yet established that they are financially sound and able to pay their bills on time. However, with careful financial planning, it may be possible for even a start-up to negotiate a trade credit deal with suppliers.

Once an enterprise is more established and has proved that it is financially sound and able to pay its bills on time, suppliers are more likely to offer trade credit.

The key benefit of trade credit for a supplier is that it encourages repeat custom.

> **KEY TERMS**
>
> **Customer:** A person or organisation that buys goods/materials or services from an enterprise.
>
> **Trade receivable:** The amount of money owed to the enterprise by customers who have had goods or services but not yet paid for them.
>
> **Goods:** The finished product sold by an enterprise to its customers.
>
> **Service:** Something that an enterprise might do for their customers (such as cleaning their windows).
>
> **Cash flow:** The movement of money in and out of the enterprise.

Trade credit between enterprises and their customers

Enterprises might also want to offer their **customers** trade credit so that they can benefit from the repeat custom that it often brings. The amount of money owed by customers is shown in the accounts as **trade receivables**.

There are downsides to offering trade credit to a customer:

1 The enterprise does not get the money for their **goods** or **service** straight away, which can cause **cash flow** problems.
2 Chasing late payments can be costly because of the extra time that takes.

> **ACTIVITY 7.1**
>
> What are the advantages and disadvantage of trade credit for:
> - an enterprise and its suppliers
> - an enterprise and its customers?

Chapter 7: The concept of trade credit

Exam-style questions

David has been baking cakes for his family and friends for as long as he can remember. Everyone loves his cakes and they are always surprised when he tells them they are low-calorie. Encouraged by his friends and family and some good market research, which shows there is a demand for low-calorie cake, David has decided to open a small bakery.

> **KEY TERM**
>
> **Materials:** The raw components (such as ingredients for a cake) that are needed to make the finished goods.

David has worked out his finances carefully and although he has enough money to buy his first order of raw **materials** (the ingredients for his cakes) he would like to keep some money aside for unexpected costs. He has spoken with a local supplier and used his detailed financial information to negotiate a trade credit deal with the supplier of his raw materials. The trade credit means that he has 30 days to pay his bill, which he is confident he can do from the revenue he brings in from selling his low-calorie cakes. He also gets to keep money in his bakery bank account for unexpected costs.

1   Define what is meant by the term 'trade credit'. [2]

2   David is starting up his own enterprise. Explain why it may be difficult for David to get a trade credit deal and what David should do to increase the likelihood of getting trade credit. [10]

3   Explain the advantages and disadvantages of trade credit for an enterprise, its suppliers and its customers. [15]

Summary

You should know:

- what trade credit means
- the differences in trade credits between an enterprise, a supplier, and a customer
- the advantages and disadvantages of credit for entrepreneurs, suppliers and customers.

Learning summary

In this chapter you will learn about:

- the importance of keeping accurate financial records
- constructing and interpreting a cash flow forecast
- calculating and explaining break even
- interpreting an income statement.

Chapter 8: Cash flow, break-even and income statement

Financial terms

In the planning stages of an enterprise it is important to accurately predict the amount of cash that flows into and out of the enterprise. To do this an enterprise will create a cash flow forecast.

> **KEY TERMS**
>
> **Break-even point:** The point at which income from sales will cover all the enterprise's costs.

It is also important to know how many units of product or services the enterprise will need to sell in order to pay all its costs. This is known as the **break-even point**.

Once the business is running, it must manage its finances by keeping records. The key record of a business is the **income** statement. The financial records of the enterprise must be true and accurate because they will be scrutinised by a variety of internal and external stakeholders (such as lenders) who will make important decisions using the information they contain. By knowing what is happening to costs, revenue and cash flow, entrepreneurs should be better placed to make the right decisions to help ensure business success.

PROJECT PROMPT

As part of your project you should create a cash flow forecast and work out the break-even point of your enterprise. They are not requirements for the coursework, but by doing this you will more accurately be able to predict the financial outcomes of your enterprise.

You can use the template at the end of this chapter to help with your forecast.

ACTIVITY 8.1

Look at the image and think about how money flows in and out of an enterprise. Create a list of the ways in which money flows into an enterprise and another list about how money flows out of an enterprise.

In →   Out →

-
-
-

-
-
-

Cash flow

A cash flow forecast uses information about all the cash that comes into an enterprise (**cash inflow**) and all the cash that goes out of an enterprise (**cash outflow**) to predict what might happen in its short term financial future. There are many reasons the enterprise will do this, including:

- to identify if the enterprise will have a **surplus** or **deficit** of cash so that plans can be put in place to resolve the situation
- to help the enterprise plan for the future, for example it can help work out when there will be enough cash in the enterprise to purchase a new piece of equipment
- to set budgets for individual departments/functions of the enterprise
- to create targets for staff and departments. The forecast is devised using assumptions that certain numbers of the product will be sold. Therefore it will provide sales staff/department performance targets. If not achieved the business may run into financial problems.

It is important to understand that although the cash flow can predict how much money is in the enterprise's bank account it does not predict the **profits** of the enterprise.

> **KEY TERMS**
>
> **Cash inflow:** Any cash that comes into the enterprise.
>
> **Cash outflow:** Any cash that goes out of the enterprise.
>
> **Surplus:** On a cash flow forecast, if the cash that comes into the enterprise is greater than the cash that goes out, there is a surplus of cash.
>
> **Deficit:** On a cash flow forecast, if the cash that comes into the enterprise is less than the cash that goes out, then there is a deficit of cash.
>
> **Profit:** When the total income of the enterprise is greater than the total expenditure of the enterprise.

MINI CASE STUDY

David's low-calorie cakes cash flow forecast

In Chapter 7 we looked at David's low-calorie cakes. One of the key financial planning documents that he created in setting up his enterprise was a cash flow forecast. His first step in working out his cash flow was to do some research into how much money he estimated he would have coming into the enterprise and what costs there would be. David worked out the following for the first six months of his enterprise.

Chapter 8: Cash flow, break-even and income statement

David's low-calorie cakes: estimated cash flow figures.

INCOME
Owner's own money (capital)	$17,000
Government grant	$2,000
Forecast monthly sales from January	$20,000

START-UP COSTS
Baking equipment	$4,000
Store fixtures and fittings	$7,000
Office equipment	$3,500
Initial marketing campaign in January	$2,500

RUNNING COSTS
Marketing from February	$1,500
Raw materials	$12,000
Part-time staff wages	$1,500
Maureen's wages	$1,500
Gas, water and electricity bills	$3,000
Opening bank balance	$0

David then gave these figures to his wife, Maureen, who was able to create a cash flow forecast of the first six months, which is given here:

Cash flow forecast for the period January to June: David's Low-calorie Cakes

	Jan	Feb	Mar	Apr	May	Jun	Total for the period
Income							
Capital	$ 17,000.00						$ 17,000.00
Grant	$ 2,000.00						$ 2,000.00
Sales revenue	$ 20,000.00	$ 20,000.00	$ 20,000.00	$ 20,000.00	$ 20,000.00	$ 20,000.00	$ 120,000.00
Total income	$ 39,000.00	$ 20,000.00	$ 20,000.00	$ 20,000.00	$ 20,000.00	$ 20,000.00	$ 139,000.00
Expenditure							
Baking equipment	$ 4,000.00						$ 4,000.00
Store fixtures and fittings	$ 7,000.00						$ 7,000.00
Office equipment	$ 3,500.00						$ 3,500.00
Marketing	$ 2,500.00	$ 1,500.00	$ 1,500.00	$ 1,500.00	$ 1,500.00	$ 1,500.00	$ 10,000.00
Raw materials	$ 12,000.00	$ 12,000.00	$ 12,000.00	$ 12,000.00	$ 12,000.00	$ 12,000.00	$ 72,000.00
Staff wages	$ 3,000.00	$ 3,000.00	$ 3,000.00	$ 3,000.00	$ 3,000.00	$ 3,000.00	$ 18,000.00
Utility bills (gas, water, electric)	$ 3,000.00	$ 3,000.00	$ 3,000.00	$ 3,000.00	$ 3,000.00	$ 3,000.00	$ 18,000.00
Total expenditure	$ 35,000.00	$ 19,500.00	$ 19,500.00	$ 19,500.00	$ 19,500.00	$ 19,500.00	$ 132,500.00
Opening bank balance	$ -	$ 4,000.00	$ 4,500.00	$ 5,000.00	$ 5,500.00	$ 6,000.00	$ -
Total income	$ 39,000.00	$ 20,000.00	$ 20,000.00	$ 20,000.00	$ 20,000.00	$ 20,000.00	$ 139,000.00
Total expenditure	$ 35,000.00	$ 19,500.00	$ 19,500.00	$ 19,500.00	$ 19,500.00	$ 19,500.00	$ 132,500.00
Closing bank balance	$ 4,000.00	$ 4,500.00	$ 5,000.00	$ 5,500.00	$ 6,000.00	$ 6,500.00	$ 6,500.00

This cash flow forecast shows that, if David's estimates are accurate, after six months of trading the enterprise should be in a surplus cash position.

Questions:
1. What period is covered by the cash flow forecast?
2. What does the column on the far right hand side of the cash flow forecast show?
3. By what amount is the closing bank balance increasing each month?
4. Would the enterprise still have a surplus after six months if David had not managed to get a $2 000 government grant?
5. What would happen to the bank balance of the enterprise if David has incorrectly estimated his monthly sales and only gets $18 000 a month?
6. Discuss possible actions David could take to improve his cash flow position.

ACTIVITY 8.2

Antoine is at school in Rwanda where he is learning about entrepreneurship. He has managed to work out his estimates for the enterprise he intends to set up as part of his course, but is not sure how to create the cash flow forecast. Put together a cash flow forecast for Antoine.

Antoine's estimates for his cash flow forecast are as follows:

INCOME:
Personal savings — RWF 109 302
Loan — RWF 54 651
Sales from January to June — RWF 98 372

START-UP COSTS:
Equipment — RWF 163 954

RUNNING COST:
Stock — RWF 54 651
Other expenses — RWF 21 860
Opening bank balance — RWF 0

Chapter 8: Cash flow, break-even and income statement

Break-even

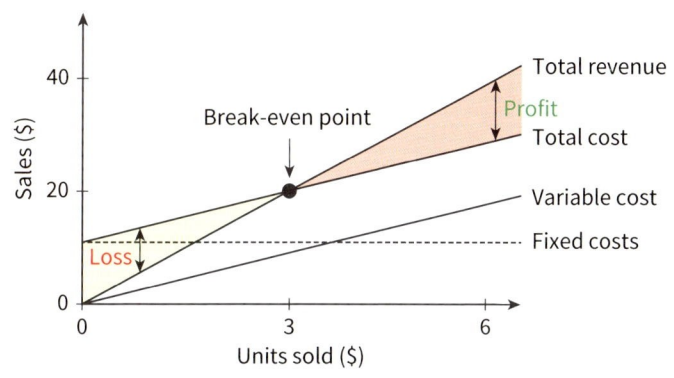

Figure 8.1: An example of a break-even chart

The break-even point is the number of units an enterprise would need to sell to be sure there is enough money coming in (revenue) to equal to all the costs of the enterprise. If the enterprise sells more units, then more money is coming in than the costs are going out, so the enterprise is making a profit (or surplus, if the enterprise is a charity). If the enterprise sells fewer units, less money is coming into the enterprise than costs going out, so the enterprise is making a **loss**.

KEY TERM

Loss: When the total income of the enterprise is less than the total expenditure of the enterprise.

To calculate the break-even point, the enterprise will need to know some key information. A start-up enterprise will need to estimate some of this information. An established enterprise would look back over past financial records to get this information.

The calculation for the break-even point is actually very simple once the enterprise knows the key information:

Fixed costs ÷ (Sales price per unit − Variable costs per unit)

This will give the number of units the enterprise needs to sell in order to break-even.

Key information	Description
Revenue	This is all the money that comes into the enterprise from selling goods or services.
Fixed costs	These are costs that stay the same no matter the activity of the enterprise. If the enterprise manufactures more products or fewer products these costs do not change. Examples of fixed costs are: • rent • business taxes • interest on loans • staff (these are employees that are not directly linked to the production of the enterprise, such as receptionists or cleaners) • insurance.
Variable costs	These are costs that increase and decrease with the activity of the enterprise. If the enterprise manufactures more products or fewer products these costs change. Examples of variable costs are: • materials • labour (these are employees that are directly linked to the production of the company, such as production line worker) • energy.
Total costs	These are all the costs of an enterprise when producing its goods or services. Fixed costs + variable costs = total costs.

Table 8.1: Information needed to calculate the break-even point

KEY TERMS

Contribution: Part of the calculation to work out break-even point:
    Contribution per unit = variable costs per unit – sale price per unit.
Cost: Cash that an enterprise spends to produce its goods or services.
Fixed costs: Costs that stay the same despite changes in the activity of the enterprise.
Variable costs: Costs that increase and decrease with the activity of the enterprise.
Total costs: The total of the variable costs + fixed costs.

ACTIVITY 8.3

Calculate the break-even point for a toy manufacturer using the following information:
Fixed costs = $5 000
Variable costs per unit = $10
Sales price per unit = $20

Chapter 8: Cash flow, break-even and income statement

Income statement

An income statement is a record of the finances of an enterprise over a specific period of time. It is produced annually to provide information to the stakeholders of the enterprise, but managers within the business may produce it more regularly for their own analyses. It shows the profit (or surplus for charities) or loss of an enterprise. In essence it shows the very simple calculation:

*Revenue – **Expenditure** = Profit or Loss*

The income statement provides useful information for various stakeholders in the enterprise:

> **KEY TERM**
>
> **Expenditure:** All the money that goes out of an enterprise.

- It gives the owners/shareholders of the enterprise a clear understanding of how much profit or loss has been made from their investment and why. This helps shareholders to understand the dividends that they will be paid out of the profits.

- It allows owners/shareholders and managers to make judgements about how well the enterprise in performing against other similar enterprises. This can also help potential investors decide whether the enterprise is worth investing in.

- It allows lenders to make judgements on whether or not the enterprise makes sufficient profits to pay back any loans. This would be done in conjunction with a cash flow forecast.

- It meets the legal obligations of certain types of enterprise where they are required to report their finances annually. For instance, the government will want to know how much profit is made so that it can work out how much tax the enterprise should pay.

- Suppliers will want to know that a firm is profitable so that they are confident that supplies will continue to be purchased and bills will be paid.

Two figures here are particularly important in analysing the enterprise: **gross profit** and **net profit**.

- Gross profit is revenue minus the cost of sales. From this figure it is possible to work out how much profit is being made from each unit of currency being spent to make the product/service.

An example of a simple income statement is given in Figure 8.2.

Hyper Music Sales	
Income statement for the year ending 31st December 2017	
Income:	
Sales revenue	$65,000.00
Cost of sales	$35,000.00
Gross profit	$30,000.00
Expenditure:	
Wages	$15,600.00
Rent	$ 2,000.00
Business tax	$ 2,100.00
Insurance	$ 1,950.00
Advertising	$ 560.00
Admin expenses	$ 500.00
Net Profit	$ 7,290.00

Figure 8.2: An example of an income statement

- Net profit is the gross profit minus all other expenditure (sometimes called **overheads**). This figure shows us what impact all other expenditure has on the profits of the enterprise, and is also the figure that shareholders are interested in because this is what their dividend (a share of the profits) is paid from.

To improve profit figures an enterprise would need to:
- increase sales revenue by either selling more or selling at a higher price
- reduce cost of sales
- reduce other expenditure (overheads).

> **KEY TERMS**
>
> **Cost of sales:** The costs that are directly linked to generating sales, such as raw materials and the labour of those directly involved in production.
>
> **Gross profit:** Revenue minus cost of sales.
>
> **Net profit:** Gross profit minus all other expenditures of the enterprise (often called overheads) that are not directly linked to generating sales.
>
> **Overheads:** Net profit minus all other expenditure.

Chapter 8: Cash flow, break-even and income statement

Exam-style questions:

Mika has a shop selling flowers. He started the enterprise 3 years ago and during this time has had a number of cash flow problems. Making a profit is important to Mika. As sales have increased, Mika would like to expand.

Mika knows that adding another shop to his enterprise would be a risk. He would have to look carefully at his financial records before preparing a business plan.

1. Define the term 'profit'. [2]
2. Identify one fixed cost and one variable cost of Mika's enterprise. [2]
3. Look back at the case study of David's Low Calorie Cakes and use this to explain the purpose of a cash flow forecast, giving examples of how it can be used by an enterprise. [10]
4. Look at the income statement. Calculate the missing figures for cost of sales and profit. [2]

Mika's florist		
Income statement for the year ending 31st December 2017		
Item	Expenditure ($)	Income ($)
INCOME		
Sales revenue		69,500.00
Cost of sales		
Gross profit		33,500.00
EXPENDITURE		
Wages	20,700.00	
Rent	7,400.00	
Business tax	5,300.00	
Insurance	1,200.00	
Advertising	850.00	
Admin expenses	1,000.00	
PROFIT/LOSS		

5. Explain two possible effects on Mika's enterprise of not keeping accurate records. [6]

Summary

You should know:

- about cash flow forecasts, break-even and income statements
- the purpose and importance of keeping accurate financial records.

Template 6: Projected income and expenditure

Items	Expenditure ($)	Income ($)
Loan/grant/start-up costs		
Income from sales		
Sale of shares (if relevant)		
Other income/investments		
TOTAL INCOME		
Rent of market space		
Raw materials (e.g. ingredients, products etc.)		
Marketing costs (e.g. advertising)		
Equipment bought/hired		
Stationery		
Loan repayment		
Other expenditure (e.g. training, security etc.)		
TOTAL EXPENDITURE		
PROFIT/LOSS (Total income *minus* total expenditure)		

Chapter 9
Marketing

Learning summary

In this chapter you will learn about:

- how marketing is used to achieve enterprise aims
- marketing from the perspective of customers
- reasons for retaining customers
- methods of measuring customer satisfaction and retention
- different methods of marketing communication and selecting appropriate methods for different enterprises
- methods of communicating marketing information to customers.

How marketing is used to achieve enterprise aims

Today **marketing** is everywhere. But what is it and why does it matter?

> **ACTIVITY 9.1**
>
> What do you understand by the term marketing and why it is used? Write down your ideas. Share them with the person next to you. Are your ideas the same or different? Why do you think this? Are there more words you can add to your list? Share your ideas with another group.
>
> As a group, produce your definition of marketing and a list of reasons why it is used.

Marketing is more than just advertising and promotion. It involves:

> **KEY TERM**
>
> **Marketing:** Anticipating, identifying and satisfying customer needs.

Identifying – finding out what customers want and need through market research.

Anticipating – what customers demand can change, so it is important to look ahead to spot the next 'big thing'. This allows an enterprise to respond more quickly to changing tastes and fashion.

Satisfying – providing products where and when they are wanted, and at a price that customers are willing to pay

An enterprise will use marketing to help it achieve its aims and to:

- raise customer awareness of the enterprise and/or products and services
- increase or maintain brand loyalty
- improve image of company
- increase or defend sales, market share or profit
- help the enterprise compete
- help the enterprise reach its target market.

Marketing also helps customers. For example:

- It provides customers with knowledge about the products so they can make more informed decisions. Customers can save time, as they don't have to search for the information they need.

- Being able to make informed decisions could save the customer money, as they don't end up buying the wrong product.
- It raises awareness of products that customers did not realise were available to buy, which allows them the opportunity to purchase if needed or wanted.
- Enterprises have to keep its customers' needs and wants in mind. This can lead to suitable products and services being made and becoming available to buy.

Customer retention

An enterprise can increase its sales by attracting new customers or keeping as many existing customers as possible. This is known as **customer retention**.

Existing customers have already shown an interest in your products and are aware of what your enterprise has to offer.

> **KEY TERM**
>
> **Customer retention:** Measuring how loyal customers are to an enterprise (and the likelihood of them buying its products or services again).

Reasons why it is important for an enterprise to retain customers

Research by Bain & Company (2011) showed that a 5 per cent increase in customer retention increases profits up to 125 per cent and a 2 per cent increase in customer retention has the same effect as decreasing costs by 10 per cent.

Finding new customers is necessary for any enterprise. However, it is important to keep existing customers because this is more cost-effective than attracting new ones. For instance:

- Marketing is expensive – from market research to promotions. If you build a relationship with customers over time, it makes it easier to provide the products required. To attract new customers, you may need to advertise in more places using more methods.
- Returning customers can provide a stable income making cash flow planning easier.
- It helps establish and maintain brand loyalty, increasing the chance of repeat business and defending sales against new competitors.
- Loyal customers tend to spend more per visit.
- Good word-of-mouth advertising, when customers recommend your products, can increase sales and potentially your market share.

ACTIVITY 9.2

Are you loyal to any particular enterprises? If so why, and if not, why not? What would make you loyal to an enterprise? Keep a note of your answers, as they may be helpful for the discussion activity later.

Methods of measuring customer satisfaction and retention

An enterprise wants customers to be satisfied with its products or services.

Knowing what customers want allows the enterprise to adapt to please its customers. It is also helpful to know the opinions of lost and potential customers to find out what it could or should do to attract/reattract their custom. However, measuring **customer satisfaction** can be difficult.

> **KEY TERM**
>
> **Customer satisfaction:** The extent to which customers are pleased with the products and services provided by an enterprise.

Methods include:

- **Number of sales.** This is a simple and quick way to measure customer satisfaction. Have sales increased or decreased? However, care is needed as changes in sales may be due to other factors, such as changes in income, tastes or competition, rather than customers being unhappy with the product or service.

- **Number of complaints and returned products.** Customers complain when they are unhappy about something. If unhappy customers tell other people about this, it can lead to a bad reputation and result in a loss of sales. Action has to be taken quickly to address the problem and prevent this. Remember that products may be returned for many reasons – the customer may not be unhappy with all aspects of the enterprise.

As well as using market research to identify potential customers, the same methods can also be used to obtain feedback from customers. For example:

- **Customer questionnaires and surveys.** These can be face-to-face, paper-based or electronic. Customers are usually asked a few short questions. When and what is asked depends on what the enterprise wants to know. An example might be how useful a website was to use when buying a product.

- **Suggestion boxes and comment cards.** Some enterprises provide simple forms or a book to complete for customers to leave feedback.
- **Mystery shopper programmes.** People act as customers to test out the service offered by a given enterprise. The 'shopper' is given a number of issues to assess and then scores the enterprise on the basis of their experience. Usually this method is organised by a specialist business and is generally only used by large enterprises because of the cost involved.
- **Focus groups.** Some enterprises want to explore the needs, thoughts and opinions of customers. Talking to the same or a similar group of people over a long period of time allows an enterprise to build up a fuller impression of what its customers think.

ACTIVITY 9.3

Design a simple customer satisfaction survey that can be used in school. Examples of possible areas to measure might include the school canteen, school shop or a specific activity, such as a trip, course or school activity.

Methods of retaining existing customers

Customers that feel valued and appreciated are more likely to remain loyal to an enterprise. This increases the chances of repeat purchases and reduces the risk of losing customers to competitors.

Ways of retaining customers include:

- offering good or improved quality products
- offering a new or wider range of products and designs
- offering good customer service by giving personal attention to the needs of customers by training employees to be helpful and knowledgeable

- providing after-sales services and support, such as offering credit facilities and delivery and product guarantees
- resolving complaints quickly and effectively with refunds or exchanges
- providing detailed information about products
- communicating regularly with customers (e.g. by using newsletters and social media
- rewarding loyalty (e.g. by offering loyalty cards, discounts, special offers and reward schemes)
- asking for feedback to find out what changes need to be made.

> **MINI CASE STUDY**
>
> ## Customer retention strategies
>
> Here are examples of customer retention strategies used by enterprises:
>
> Tom's Shoes have a 'One for One' policy. For every pair of shoes that are purchased, they give a pair to people in need, donating over 60 million pairs of new shoes.
>
> Starbucks used sounds and smells in their coffee shop to improve the customer experience. Today they use technology. One innovative way to help customer retention is a mobile 'Order & Pay' feature within their app. This means that when you arrive at Starbucks your order is there and ready to collect.
>
> **Questions:**
>
> 1 Think about local enterprises you know or visit. Individually, make a note of which methods they use to try to retain customers. If they do not use any, why do you think this is?
>
> 2 Share your information with the others in the group. Is one method used most often? Do the methods vary depending on the type of enterprise? Which method would work for you (look back at your notes from the earlier activity on retention)?

Chapter 9: Marketing

MINI CASE STUDY

Gabriel's food stall

Gabriel has a food stall at a busy market selling hot and cold drinks. He has noticed that 40 per cent of his customers visit his stall every week to buy his products. Gabriel would like to be able to retain more of his customers.

Questions:

1. Explain two possible reasons why retaining customers might be important to Gabriel's business.
2. Explain one advantage and one disadvantage for Gabriel of introducing a reward card.
3. Explain two methods of customer retention that Gabriel could use. Which method do you think Gabriel should use, and why?

Methods of marketing communication to reach intended customers

Advertising can be informative or persuasive. Informative advertising gives customers information about products and services. Persuasive methods are designed to attract attention and convince customers that they need its products.

> **KEY TERM**
>
> **Justify:** Support a case with evidence/argument.

An enterprise will use a variety of methods to ensure both potential and existing customers are aware of its products and to encourage them to buy.

PROJECT PROMPT

There is no need to include a marketing plan or discuss other elements of the marketing mix, such as price or product, in your project. Simply focus on marketing communication. This includes posters, online and printed advertisements.

For all marketing methods it is important to think about the message, and where and how it will be distributed.

Method	Advantages	Disadvantages
Leaflets and flyers	Simple, easy and cheap to produce Can be kept for future reference	Often seen as junk mail so ignored or thrown away Pollution issue caused by litter
Posters and billboards	Good visual impact Can be seen numerous times as people pass Can target people in a given location	Easy to miss as only seen for a few seconds as people pass No detailed information Can be easily damaged
Online communication and social media	Can have two-way communication with customers Can be accessed in most countries so larger potential audience Sites easy to update and maintain	People must have internet access to use Easy to ignore or block out adverts Can be easy to miss especially as large number of sites and platforms exist
Sponsorship	Association with another party can increase awareness amongst target market	Negative publicity can affect both parties Cost of sponsorship can be high
Newspapers (local, regional or national)	Can reach large numbers of people at same time Can be kept for future reference	Can be expensive depending on size and position of advert, and if it is in colour or black or white. Not everyone reads newspapers
Television	Can reach large numbers of people By selecting certain times and programmes can target audiences Colour, sound and motion helps attract attention	Expensive to produce advert and pay television company to show Cannot change message easily Relatively easy to ignore or skip adverts by changing channel
Radio	Can be used to target particular audiences or areas Cheaper than television	Only have sound to attract attention Advert has to be remembered as no document to refer to

Table 9.1: Advantages and disadvantages of different methods of marketing communication

Method	Advantages	Disadvantages
Cinema	Uses sound, colour and motion to create impact Potential customers can be targeted by film shown	Target market likely to be small People may only see advert once High cost to produce and show advert
Magazines	Can be used to target a local or national, specialist audience	Can be expensive based on choice of magazine, size of advert and if colour is used
Newsletters (printed and electronic)	Can be used to provide regular updates to customers about its products Can be posted to individuals, delivered to a whole area, or placed for people to collect	Customers may be unwilling to provide contact details Target market may not read newsletters Time and cost to produce on a regular basis
Word of mouth	Free, personal and honest feedback	No control over what customers say
Announcements	Relatively simple to arrange Can target people in a given location	Target market likely to be small Not everyone listens

Table 9.1: (*Continued*)

ACTIVITY 9.4

Think about the adverts you have seen recently on television, billboards and posters. If possible, make a record of all the type of adverts you see over the course of a few days.

For each one, write down what the product was, when and where it was shown.

What do you like about the advert and why? Is there anything you would change and why? Would it encourage you to buy the product? Why?

What is the difference between the marketing communications seen on television and on billboards? Can you think of reasons for this? Which do you prefer? Why?

(Note: You can repeat this activity with different methods of marketing communication.)

The growth of electronic media has opened up new ways of communicating with customers. Websites, social media, online videos, SMS text messages, apps, viral campaigns, blogs and **sponsored** links are just the start.

KEY TERM

Sponsorship: An enterprise paying or offering something in return for having its name linked with an event, person or group.

> **ACTIVITY 9.5**
>
> What methods of social media can you name? Which ones do you use? Why?

Most enterprises will use a variety of methods. For all methods it is important to think about the message, specifically where and how it will be distributed.

> **ACTIVITY 9.6**
>
> Asha has a market stall selling key rings and stationery. She decides to carry out some market research to identify new products. The results suggest a high demand for cell (mobile) phone cases. She has to decide on a suitable method of marketing communication to use to inform customers about the new product.
>
> Design a poster or leaflet that Asha could use to promote her enterprise. (Hint: think about what and how much information to include, who the target market is, and where/how she is going to display or distribute it.)

> **PROJECT PROMPT**
>
> Whether you are working individually or as part of a group, try to create your own examples of different marketing communication for your enterprise project.
>
> Although the examples are not assessed, they can still be used as evidence of skills, such as creativity, or commented on when evaluating marketing communications used.

Methods including television, radio, cinema, newspaper and magazines, posters and billboards, leaflets and internet are sometimes referred to as mass media advertising. This is because they are designed to reach a large number of people.

These are just a few of the many methods used for marketing communication. Other examples include direct mail, word-of-mouth and announcements. Word of mouth is an unpaid form of promotion in which customers tell other people about an enterprise, product or service. An announcement is a formal public statement used to provide people with information. Telling people about a product personally may seem old-fashioned, but it is still an effective method of communication. When satisfied customers tell friends about a product they like or about an announcement they have heard, the message is still being passed on.

> **TIP**
>
> If you use announcements for your project, make sure you prepare a script and include a copy of it as part of your evidence.

Chapter 9: Marketing

Which marketing method?

There is no best method. Each option has its advantages and disadvantages. It is important to choose the right method to ensure you get your message across to your target audience.

Factors to consider include:

- the cost of method
- how much money is available to spend
- how many potential customers can be reached
- ease of distribution
- who the target audience is
- the type of product
- the actions of competitors.

Some methods are not available to every enterprise. For example, start-up enterprises are likely to have less money available so will have to select cheaper options than larger established organisations to ensure it can cover other costs.

If the product or service is aimed at young people, social media could be a better option than advertising in a newspaper that they are unlikely to read.

What is being sold can also influence the method used. For example, an enterprise selling specialist cooking equipment may choose to use food magazines as these are likely to be read by its specific target market.

> **PROJECT PROMPT**
>
> For your project, try to select no more than three or four marketing options. There is no need to discuss more. This is because it is important to provide detailed explanations to do well in this task (see Chapter 13). Remember that it is highly unlikely that methods such as cinema or television would be suitable for a school-based project.
>
> When explaining your options, do not simply list generic advantages and disadvantages of each option. This does not demonstrate application or analysis. For each method, try to explain why it may be suitable (or not) for your enterprise project. Consider factors (selection criteria) such as what you are selling, whom you are selling to, and cost. Remember to include clear reasons to support your final choice, and explain why the other options were rejected.

Any marketing communications used must meet legal obligations for marketing and selling. This includes ensuring that any descriptions or statements about your products and services are true and do not mislead customers.

ACTIVITY 9.7

For each of the following scenarios identify three possible methods of communication that the enterprises could use. Decide which of the methods they should use. Give reasons for your choice.

- A leading international food retailer wants to start selling its electronic goods in your country.
- A small enterprise selling t-shirts wants to inform customers about its latest designs.

PROJECT PROMPT

As part of your project, you will be required to give a short individual presentation outlining your proposed methods of marketing communication, with reasons. The material for this is the three or four marketing methods you have just researched and written about. The purpose of the presentation is to assess your communication, and, potentially, your enterprise skills. For example, it could include being creative in how you deliver your presentation, or showing how creative you were when in the options discussed. There is an opportunity to gain credit for this or other skills shown in this task as well.

Try to use slides and include examples of your proposed methods. When explaining your choices, make it clear how or why these methods would help your enterprise reach the potential market and help attract customers. For example, say why the leaflet or posts on social media are suitable for what you want to sell.

TIP

In the presentation, you will be assessed on your enterprise and communication skills. Make sure you practise how and what you are going to say beforehand. This can also help you be less nervous when you do the actual presentation.

Chapter 9: Marketing

Exam-style questions

Gaston wants to set up a 'garden tidy' business in his local town. His market research shows there is likely to be high demand for this service, especially from people over the age of 50 and people with families. His research also shows that if he can offer a good customer service this would help customer retention.

Gaston has identified three possible marketing methods he could use: leaflets, advert in local paper or social media.

1. Define 'customer retention'. [2]
2. Explain **two** methods Gaston could use for retaining customers. [6]
3. Explain **two** factors that Gaston should consider when deciding which method of marketing communication to use. [6]
4. Evaluate the effectiveness of the marketing methods used in your enterprise project. [15]
5. Recommend which one of the following marketing methods Gaston should use to tell people about his enterprise: local newspapers, a leaflet or social media. Justify your answer. [15]

Summary

You should know:

- marketing communication is the way an enterprise makes its products and services known to its target market
- each method has its advantages and disadvantages
- how marketing is used to achieve enterprise aims
- how marketing works from the perspective of customers
- reasons for retaining customers
- methods of measuring customer satisfaction and retention
- different methods of marketing communication and selecting appropriate methods for different enterprises
- there are many factors to consider when choosing a suitable method of marketing communication.

116

Chapter 10
Negotiation

Learning summary

In this chapter you will learn about:

- negotiation
- the stages in the negotiation process.

The purpose and role of negotiation

We all need or want things – permission to do things or go to places, information, access to resources, cheaper prices, more wages. Others have needs as well and sometimes this can fit with what we want and sometimes it can't. Others will sometimes want us to do or offer something in exchange for what we want. The terms of the transaction – what and how much – can be discussed. **Negotiation** is all about trying to find a solution that everyone is happy with.

> **KEY TERM**
>
> **Negotiation:** The process of discussion in order to reach agreement on a course of action (or solve a dispute) that satisfies the interests of all involved.

The process of negotiation can involve:

- resolving disputes
- agreeing on courses of action
- bargaining for individual or collective advantage
- reaching outcomes to satisfy the interests of those involved.

There are three main stages in a negotiation:

1 Planning

2 Conducting the negotiation

3 Measuring success

Planning a negotiation

You cannot predict what is going to happen in the negotiation. Having a clear focus can help you stay calm whatever happens in the meeting.

Planning involves two main stages: setting objectives and identifying benefits and drawbacks of a proposal.

Setting objectives

Thinking ahead is important to a successful negotiation.

Ask yourself the following questions:

- What do you want to achieve from the negotiation?
- What do you think the other side (person or organisation) wants?
- What are you going to say and how are you going to say it?
- Who are you going to be negotiating with?

Chapter 10: Negotiation

- What will you do if you cannot get your first choice? What are you prepared to accept, offer or give up to reach a compromise agreement?
- Will you insist on getting exactly what you want or are you willing to collaborate with the other side to find an alternative solution?
- Have you listed the consequences for both sides if your proposal is not accepted?
- At what point would you walk away from the negotiation, and why?

The answers to these questions will influence your negotiating strategy.

Possible outcomes

- A collaborative approach can often provide the best result as it aims to achieve a **win-win** outcome. This is where both sides gain something from the process.
- Some negotiations will end in a compromise agreement (also known as **win-lose/lose-win**) with both sides getting a slightly different outcome than originally intended.
- If you adopt a competitive approach (win-lose) you must be sure you are right and the other side has no choice but to accept your proposal. If you are not willing to compromise at all you must be prepared to leave the meeting with nothing (**lose-lose**).

ACTIVITY 10.1

Try this simple activity to show the effect of different strategies.

Divide people into A and B. Ask the A's to leave the room. While outside, explain the activity to the B's. When the A's re-enter the room, each B pairs up with an A and asks their partner to raise their arms so that the palms of their hands are facing them.

Round 1: All the B's start pushing their partners without any explanation to try and get them to go to the opposite side of the room.

Round 2: Repeat the start position. This time, B asks A to accompany them to the other side of the room, giving a reason for the move.

As a group, discuss how different people feel after each round.

TIP

Do not ask for something that you know the other side will not accept in a negotiation. If you do, there is little or no scope for discussion and you are unlikely to be successful.

MINI CASE STUDY

Keely and Jacob's popcorn

Keely and Jacob make popcorn, which they sell at local festivals. Both Keely and Jacob have been surprised at how popular their product is. To increase output, Keely wants a popcorn machine, saying 'Everyone wants popcorn! If we are to meet demand we cannot keep making it by hand.' Looking at some market research Jacob agrees, but thinks they should negotiate a lease for the machine.

The situation: Ideally Jacob wants a new machine on a month's free trial. Afterwards, he would like to lease it for a one-year period rather than the usual two years. He wants the machine company to be responsible for all repairs and do any repair work within 24 hours.

However, he would also accept a discounted rental fee for the trial period. Alternatively, he would be prepared to sign a lease which would allow him to return the machine at the end of the month without a penalty, should he decide he does not want or cannot afford it. He could be prepared to accept a used machine to see if it is sensible for him to invest in a new machine.

Choosing evidence to use

Any information used must be accurate, well presented and include all the relevant facts. For example, if you are asking for finance the other party is likely to want to see a business plan or cash flow forecasts to check if you are able to repay the money. Giving samples of poor-tasting food is unlikely to convince someone to give you permission to sell your food from their market stall or shop.

> **Example:** Jacob may find it helpful to research the costs of buying and leasing machinery from other machine companies. This can also act as a guide as to what is a reasonable amount to pay so he does not end up paying more than necessary.

Benefits and weaknesses of a proposal

Write down possible advantages and disadvantages for both sides of accepting your proposal. Try to identify what they may want in return for an agreement and any reasons why they may or may not accept your proposal.

Try to provide evidence to support each point made. For example, market research data can show potential demand and financial projections can support pricing and costing decisions.

> **Example:** Jacob thinks that letting him have the machinery on a free trial would allow him time to see if his market research data about expected demand is correct.

Arguments and counter arguments for the proposal

The other side may put forward reasons that go against some or all points you plan to make as part of your case.

Identify key details that you think the other side may disagree with. Think about why they may be opposed to it so you can be ready with a suitable response.

If you cannot think of a suitable answer it may be that what you are proposing is unreasonable. You still have time to change parts of your proposal if necessary.

> **For example:**
>
> **Detail:** Jacob believes that letting him have the machinery on a free trial would allow him time to see if his market research data about expected demand is correct.
>
> **Counter argument:** The company may not want to offer the machinery on a free loan as it could be losing potential revenue by leasing the machinery to someone else for a fee.
>
> **Jacob's reply:** If I find out that the demand is correct, I will be able to sell more popcorn and may be able to purchase more machines from you.

Template of a plan for negotiation

The situation:
To agree terms to lease a popcorn machine — *State the purpose of the negotiation*

PEOPLE INVOLVED AND DATE OF NEGOTIATION:
- Jacob
- Sales manager from the machine company.

BENEFITS AND DRAWBACKS OF ACCEPTING MY PROPOSAL:

Benefits:
Would allow me to to increase output which may lead to additional requests for machinery — *Explain the advantages or reasons why the other side should support your proposal*

Drawbacks:
Machine company may not be able to afford to loan the machine without charging a fee — *Explain the disadvantages or why the other side may not support your proposal*

OUTCOME OF MEETING:
This section can only be completed after the negotiation has taken place. Make a record of the deal agreed.

Figure 10.1: A negotiation plan

> **PROJECT PROMPT**
>
> You will be required to plan and conduct a negotiation as part of your project. What this is for will depend entirely on what you need. For example, it may be obtaining permission from school, asking parents or someone else for money or equipment. The important thing is that it is relevant.

Chapter 10: Negotiation

> **ACTIVITY 10.2**
>
> Abdul has to make something in order to enter a school competition. Using his grandmother's recipe, he starts producing homemade lemonade. Afterwards his friends all ask him to make some for them. Demand increases quickly and Abdul plans to open a Saturday market stall. Adbul needs permission from the school to be allowed to apply for the stall.
>
> Write down possible benefits and drawbacks of Abdul's proposal.

Skills required for a negotiation

Persuasion

Good communication skills are an important part of being a successful negotiator. As with all skills, practice is important as it can take time to develop effective skills. Try some of the following activities to help you develop your negotiation skills.

You will need to be able to explain points in clear and simple language, and do so with confidence.

> **ACTIVITY 10.3**
>
> This activity is good practice for your presentation of your project.
>
> Imagine a visitor from another planet has arrived at your school. They know nothing about life on Earth and are looking for an interesting item to take back as a souvenir. You have been shortlisted to suggest a suitable item.
>
> Choose an item you like (e.g. your mobile phone, a piece of clothing or a favourite food treat). Explain the benefits of this item, share your enthusiasm for it and try to convince them that this is the item they should choose.
>
> You have five minutes to prepare a two-minute talk.
>
> In your negotiation you need to be able to show you are interested in what you are doing. Repeat the activity with an item that you do not like. Can you show the same level of knowledge and enthusiasm?

Listening

Listening skills are also important. If you do not know what the other side has said, you cannot ask the right questions and may miss out on important information to help you reach a successful outcome.

ACTIVITY 10.4

In pairs, one person reads out a funny poem or short story. The other person has to listen carefully, without taking notes, and must then repeat the story back to them.

The aim is to remember accurately as many important details as possible, in the right order. Swap roles and repeat with a different poem or story.

Depending on what is being discussed, who is involved and how the negotiation goes, you may also need to use other skills, including problem-solving, decision-making, and initiative to reach a favourable agreement (see Chapter 2).

TIP

It is important to practise your skills and strategy as often as you can before you take part in the formal negotiation for your project when implementing your plan. It could be in shops, with friends or family as well as at school. What you negotiate over and where does not matter.

ACTIVITY 10.5

Take a simple everyday object, such as a spoon, pen or an apple.

Set a time limit, for example an hour or a day.

Can you persuade someone to accept your object in exchange for something that they have? Don't stop at one negotiation. Once you have successfully negotiated a swap, can you then exchange the new item for something else? How many successful negotiations can you manage in the time available?

Keep a note of the strategies you used. Which ones worked, and which ones were less successful?

TIP

Remember, haggling is not the same as negotiation. An effective negotiation is when both sides are happy with the outcome.

Conducting the negotiation

Setting the tone

It is important to create the right atmosphere in which it is easy for everyone to listen to each other and work together.

- **When and where.** Find a suitable time and location for the meeting. Allow enough time for everyone to ask all the questions they need. Try to prepare an agenda (we'll look at this more in Chapter 11). A clear structure allows both sides to have a better idea about what to expect, which can help achieve a favourable outcome.

- **Get to know the other side.** Do not go straight into the negotiation. Look for ways to build trust so that they (and you) feel more at ease. Listen and be interested in what they have to say. This can also help you decide on your negotiation strategy.

- **Language.** What you say and how you say it are both important. Use clear and simple language and try to avoid jargon. The words you use, how you dress and your body language can influence how the other person will respond to you. Try to act and look as if you want to achieve a successful outcome to the negotiation.

- **Be confident and calm.** Do not let others see that you may be nervous. Relax and remember what you want to achieve. If there are times in the meeting when you do not know what to do or say next, create time to think by asking a question. For example, 'Can I just check …?' or 'If I did this, what would you do?'

Presenting your proposal

Explain simply and clearly to the other side what you want and what you are willing to offer them and why they should accept your proposal.

Be specific – only use information and materials that are relevant to your proposal.

If you are using visual aids, handouts or slides, print enough copies for everyone. Check that any equipment you need is available and that it works.

Understanding other points of view

You need to get the other side to share their requirements with you. The best way to do this is to ask questions to clarify points and find out what the other side want or are willing to accept from you. You may need to offer and accept changes to your first choice option to reach an agreement. This is called bargaining – 'give and take'.

Remember to listen as well. Do not simply keep talking. You also need to know what the other person is thinking so you can plan what to do or say next.

Summarising to check understanding

Make sure you are clear about what you and the other side are offering. Ask more questions and listen carefully to the responses to confirm your understanding.

Remember, you can always reject the deal and walk away if you think the terms are unreasonable.

Reaching an agreement

When both sides are happy with what is being proposed, you can finalise the deal. Put down in writing what has been agreed so everyone knows what has been decided for future reference.

> **ACTIVITY 10.6**
>
> This simple activity will allow you to practise your negotiation skills and strategy.
>
> Cut up some pictures (or playing cards) into four quarters. (Allow four pictures per group of four people). Mix up all the pieces and share them equally between every group. Each team has a short amount of time to identify which pieces they have and what they need to complete their pictures. Allow everyone between ten and 15 minutes to negotiate with the other groups. The aim is for each group to try to persuade the other groups to swap pieces with them so the group can complete as many of the pictures as possible.
>
> The team with the most completed pictures wins.

> **PROJECT PROMPT**
>
> Keep a record of how the negotiation goes and what skills you use for your project. Remember, the outcome of your negotiation does not have to be successful. You only need to be able to show how you applied the named skills. If you can explain why you were not good at negotiation this can still be used as valid evidence.

Measuring success

The purpose of this stage is to identify what went well and to consider how you could improve next time.

There are many ways to look at success. Do not judge success only on the outcome ('Did I achieve my objective?') but also think about the process ('How did I achieve my objective?').

There is a wide range of evidence you can use, such as the amount, cost or price paid, feedback received from a third party or some form of self-assessment.

The following questions might be helpful to you when you are measuring your success.

Outcome:

- Did you get what you wanted? Was the other side happy with the outcome? How do you know or why do you think this?
- If the negotiation was unsuccessful, why do you think this?

Process:

- How well did you do when planning and conducting the negotiation?
- Had you anticipated their counter arguments?
- Did you manage to set the right tone?
- Did you use simple and clear language? Did you ask the right questions? Did you listen carefully to the points and arguments made by other side?
- Did you manage to persuade them to change their point of view? How did you achieve this?
- Would you change your negotiation strategy next time?
- Which enterprise skills did you use?

> **PROJECT PROMPT**
>
> The success or failure of the negotiation can be an issue for discussion in your project (see Chapter 13.) These prompts can provide a basis for your analysis and evaluation.

Choose criteria that are suitable for you and your enterprise project. Not all these questions will be appropriate for every negotiation.

> **TIP**
>
> There is a lot of information in this chapter. When you do your negotiation, the key things to remember are:
> - Know your objective – why are you here?
> - Prepare – know the benefits and weaknesses of your proposal, and have potential solutions ready.
> - Be an effective negotiator – this means listen carefully, be willing to compromise if necessary and stay calm – don't rush into a decision.

Exam-style questions

Milo plans to open a market stall selling burgers and hot dogs. Milo knew there would be many other stalls selling food there. Being able to set competitive prices would be important for Milo's enterprise.

Milo has arranged a meeting with a local supplier. He knows he will have to spend time preparing for the negotiation so he can agree a suitable price for the ingredients he needs.

1. Define 'negotiation'. [2]

2. Identify **three** questions Milo should consider when planning for the negotiation. [3]

3. Explain **two** ways that Milo could help ensure a successful outcome for his negotiation. [6]

4. Milo prepared to negotiate with the supplier. Using examples from your enterprise project, discuss how you tried to ensure a successful outcome for your negotiation. [10]

Chapter 10: Negotiation

Summary

You should know:

- negotiations take place every day for a variety of reasons
- good planning and effective negotiation skills can help achieve a successful outcome
- the key to an effective negotiation is planning, preparation and practice
- not all negotiations will be successful
- the review process is important to help you prepare better for future negotiations.

Learning summary

In this chapter you will learn about:

- preparing for, running and recording a meeting
- using slides, handouts and visual aids in a presentation
- writing a formal report.
- when formal and informal communications are appropriate.
- the impact of non-verbal communications on the message being communicated.

Chapter 11: Communication

Types of communication

Good communication is essential for the efficient functioning of any enterprise. When done properly it is the process through which the **sender** passes their message to a **receiver** so that it is accurately understood and can be acted upon.

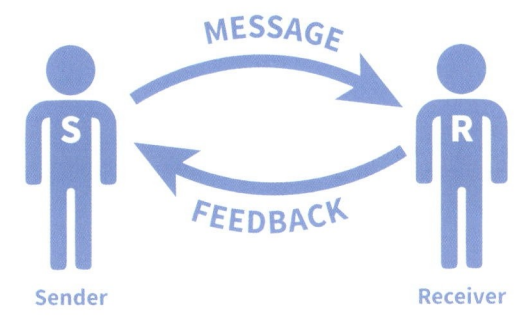

Figure 11.1: The message and feedback loop

> **KEY TERMS**
>
> **Sender:** An organisation/group/individual attempting to get their message to others.
>
> **Receiver:** An organisation/group/individual to whom a message is sent.
>
> **Audience:** The organisation/group/individual that you are communicating with.
>
> **Informal:** Relaxed, friendly and unofficial.
>
> **Formal:** Conventional, polite, respectful and official.
>
> **Slang:** Words or phrases that might be used when chatting with family or friends informally.
>
> **Jargon:** Special words or phrases that are used by a particular group or industry that are not commonly used by everybody.

Communication can happen in a variety of ways, including written, verbal and non-verbal methods, and in a variety of media such as emails, telephone calls and video conferencing. When communicating, an enterprise needs to consider the **audience** it communicates with and decide whether the language and media used need to be formal or **informal**.

Formal written and verbal communication

An enterprise will communicate formally when they are communicating something that is official, or with an organisation, group or individual who they should show respect.

Formal written communications should be polite and respectful and written using conventional spelling, punctuation and grammar; there should be no **slang** and little **jargon** because this may lead to misunderstandings. For example, any slang that you use with your friends may not be understood outside your friendship group, and jargon is usually used within a particular industry so anyone who isn't working in that industry may not understand what is meant. Some examples of official written communication that an enterprise would write formally are:

- reports – such as a progress report on a project
- letters – such as a letter sent with a contract to supply goods or services
- emails – any emails sent concerning the enterprise should be written formally.

Formal verbal communications should be polite and respectful. Again, there should be no slang and little jargon. Some example of verbal communication that and enterprise should do formally are:

- job interviews
- negotiations
- meetings.

Non-verbal communication

Non-verbal communication can have a big impact upon verbal communications when both the sender and receiver can see each other. Non-verbal communications are wordless clues that the receiver can pick up on that will either:

- reinforce the message that the sender is trying to communicate because it will be positive and give the receiver the impression that the sender is enthusiastic and cares about their message
- confuse the message that the sender is trying to communicate because it will be negative and give the receiver the impression that the sender is not really supportive and engaged with their message.

Non-verbal communication includes body language, proximity, touch, personal appearance, environmental appearance, voice intonation and voice volume. Table 11.1 shows some general guidelines for good non-verbal communication. However, these may vary slightly depending upon the culture of those communicating.

Chapter 11: Communication

Type of non-verbal communication:	Impact on formal communication:	
	Reinforcing the message	Confusing the message
Body language	Stand straight/sit up straight facing the audience Making eye contact with a smiling face Slow deliberate gestures	Slouching/leaning, facing away from the audience Looking away/at the ground with minimal facial expression
Proximity	Standing face-to-face, an arm's length apart	Standing less than an arm's length apart
Touch	Holding your hand out for a handshake	Any other physical contact!
Personal appearance	Well-groomed Smart clothes	Poorly groomed Casual clothes
Environment appearance	Neat and tidy	Messy and uncared for
Voice intonation	Multi-tonal – bright, positive, and cheerful	Monotone
Voice volume	Audible	Too quiet or too loud
Voice clarity	Clear to make out every word Slow enough that the audience can keep up and take on all the information	Mumbled Rushed so that the audience does not have time to take everything in

Table 11.1: Types of non-verbal communication and its impact on formal communication

PROJECT PROMPT

In your project you will need to produce reports and presentations using formal verbal and non-verbal communication.

Informal communication

Informal communication is used when communicating with family and friends. Sometimes within an enterprise co-workers will communicate informally when it is not official. In informal communication it is more acceptable to use slang, and non-verbal communication is much more relaxed. Some examples of when informal communication is acceptable in an enterprise are:

- emails can also be informal if the subject is not related to the enterprise, such as emailing a co-worker to arrange to meet for lunch
- co-workers having a chat over lunch about life outside work
- an informal meeting with co-workers to come up with ideas in preparation for a formal meeting.

ACTIVITY 11.1

In an enterprise there are times when you should use formal communication and other times when you can use informal communication. Read through these situations and state whether you would use formal or informal communications.

- You have been asked to attend a meeting with your suppliers to negotiate a cheaper deal.
- You are meeting with your manager to discuss a potential promotion.
- Your friend works in a different department of the same enterprise. You are going to meet them at lunch time to catch up on all the gossip.

Meetings, presentations and reports

In enterprise, a meeting is when people come together for a particular purpose. Getting a group of people together can be a great way to tackle some tasks, like weighing up alternatives, generating ideas, tackling problems, and making decisions. It is also a way of clearly communicating with people. However, if a meeting isn't well managed there can be arguments, or people may be intimidated so that they don't say what they are thinking.

There are lots of reasons why an enterprise might want to hold a meeting.

- **Managing a project.** Projects tend to require meetings at various stages to ensure that it stays on track and is completed on schedule.

Chapter 11: Communication

- **Managing people.** Many enterprises have regularly scheduled meetings. Known as 'standing meetings', they provide a chance to review the work accomplished for example, in the previous week and look ahead to brief staff on what needs to be accomplished in the coming week.

- **Working with a customer.** Many types of enterprise, especially those providing a service, will have regular meetings to support the ongoing customer relationship.

- **Other methods of communication are becoming complex.** Sometimes communications that take place using email and social media chat become increasingly complex and confusing. When this happens it can be time to call a meeting so that a conversation can take place to clear up the communication.

- **Problems are arising.** If a project is going wrong, people are not working together well or an emergency occurs, it's time to call a meeting to make decisions that will sort the problem out.

- **Training people.** It is often cheaper and quicker to get a group of people together to train them in how to do something. This also means that the training is consistent.

- **Conferences.** Enterprises like to hold a conference on a particular issue to share information and new ideas to those who attend.

Organising a meeting

The first thing to think about is why you are calling the meeting and what the desired outcome of the meeting should be. Knowing this will help you to create two key documents; the notice of meeting, and the agenda.

The notice of meeting is just an invite to attend the meeting. The notice is usually sent via letter or email. On the notice there should be:

- the date, time, duration and venue of the meeting
- the purpose of the meeting and its expected outcome
- the instructions on how to accept or decline the invitation.

When people have accepted the invitation to attend the meeting they are sent the agenda along with any other documents that they are required to read before the meeting. As a general rule this should all be sent at least 5 working days before the meeting.

An agenda usually includes the following information:

- general – the date, time, venue and duration of the meeting.

- the attendee list – it is a good idea to list the people attending the meeting. You should also list **apologies**, which is all the people who were invited but could not attend.

- the **minutes** of the last meeting – if there was a meeting before this one it is important that the last meeting's minutes are agreed by everyone and people have a chance to give an update if they were previously allocated a job to do.

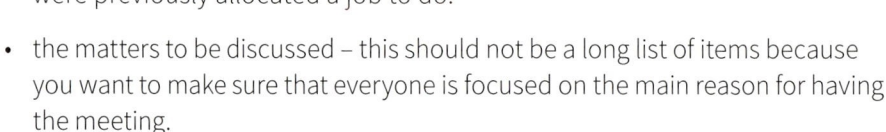

> **KEY TERMS**
>
> **Apologies:** An item on the minutes of a meeting which shows the people who were invited to attend, but unable to do so.
>
> **Minutes:** A document giving a clear and accurate record of the meeting.

- the matters to be discussed – this should not be a long list of items because you want to make sure that everyone is focused on the main reason for having the meeting.

- any other business (AOB) – this is an opportunity for people to bring up small items they would like everyone to know about. It is not time for them to add an extra matter to be discussed. New matters to be discussed should be kept for the next meeting.

- the date and time of next meeting – if there is a need to organise another meeting it is often easier to organise the next meeting with everybody present.

Figure 11.2 is an example of an agenda your enterprise teacher might get for a meeting.

Enterprise faculty meeting

Date: 28th August 2018
Time/duration: 1.30pm – 3.00pm
Venue: Meeting room 11

Agenda:
1. Attendees list: JT, MB and MP
2. Minutes of the previous meeting
3. Items for discussion
    a. Report on progress of students
    b. Appointment of Enterprise Support Assistant
4. Any other business
5. Date and time of next meeting

Figure 11.2: An example of a meeting agenda

Being prepared for a meeting is important because it will help the meeting to run smoothly and make it more likely to achieve the desired outcome of the meeting.

Key roles in a meeting

In the meeting, two key roles need to be undertaken: the role of chairperson and the role of minute taker.

- Chairperson – makes sure the meeting stays on track and achieves the desired outcome. They should set the rules for the meeting to make sure that everyone has a chance to voice their opinion and be part of the decisions that need to be made. They also have to make sure that people don't spend too long discussing one matter on the agenda so that other items don't get talked about.
- Minute taker – records a summary of the discussion that takes place during the meeting, especially the decisions that are made during the meeting and if anyone is allocated a task to do after the meeting. Once the meeting is over the minute taker will need to type up the discussion, decisions and jobs allocated in the meeting. These minutes are then sent out to all the people who attended

the meeting so that everybody has a record of what was discussed, what decisions were made and what jobs have to be done and by whom.

Figure 11.3 is an example of minutes from a faculty meeting that your enterprise teacher might have attended.

ENTERPRISE FACULTY MEETING

Minutes of meeting

Date: 28th August 2018
Time: 1.30pm – 3.00pm
Venus: Meeting room 11

Present:
MP – Head of faculty for Enterprise
MB – Teacher of Enterprise

It is a good idea to record when people were invited but were not able to attend.

If something from a previous meeting was dealt with it should be recorded.

Agenda Item	Action
Apologies • JT	
Minutes of the previous meeting • Agreed (MP to send to admin for filing)	MP
Matters arising from the previous meeting • MB stated that he had met with the head teacher and agreed additional funding for rewards trips.	
Report on progress of students • MP thanked MB for providing data on his classes prior to the meeting. • MP explained his analysis of the data. • MB agreed to run more after-school workshops to help improve grades in the run up to coursework deadlines.	MB
Appointment of Enterprise Support Assistant • MP thanked MB for writing the person specification and job description. • MP asked MB if he would like to interview the candidates. MB agreed. • MP to observe candidates in classroom situation.	MB MP
Another other business • None	
Date and time of next meeting • 30th October 2018, 4.30pm	

A general summary of the discussion and any decisions made.

Shows where someone has been given a job to do.

Figure 11.3: An example of meeting minutes

Attending a meeting

The organisers of a meeting should send you a notice of the meeting. It will give enough information that you can check that you are able to attend the meeting and will know why you need to attend the meeting. You will need to let the meeting organiser know that you accept their invitation to attend, or you will need to decline the invitation and give a reason why you're unable to make it.

About five working days before the meeting you should receive all the documentation for the meeting, such as the agenda. You can refer back to Figure 11.2 to see an example of an agenda for a meeting. You may also receive other documents, which you are expected read and understand before the meeting because they will support the discussions that take place in the meeting. Sometimes you are even given a short task to prepare before the meeting.

As an attendee of the meeting it is your responsibility to turn up on time, participate in the discussions and help with making any decision in the politest way possible whilst remembering that everyone's opinion is important.

Evaluating a meeting

Entrepreneurs need to think about how successful their meetings are. Meetings take up valuable time and if they are not achieving the desired outcomes, that time has been wasted. There are some key indicators of a successful meeting:

- No one person dominated the discussion. Everyone contributed to the discussion and valued the opinions of each other.
- All agenda items were discussed, decisions were made, and everyone knows what is expected of them after the meeting (for example, someone might have been given a job to do before the next meeting). Refer back to Figure 11.3 to see an example of minutes from a meeting, which clearly document what was discussed and the jobs given to certain people as actions from the meeting.
- The meeting did not over-run its allocated time.

If the meeting was not successful it is important to understand:

- what the problem in the meeting was
- why that problem occurred in the meeting
- possible solutions to prevent the problem from reoccurring in the future.

Table 11.2 gives some possible problems that occur in meetings, a likely reason and a potential solution:

Problem	Reason	Solution
One person dominates discussion.	They are the only one prepared for the meeting.	Make sure that everyone has the meeting documents at least five days before the meeting and know how important it is to read the documents before the meeting.
	The chairperson is not managing the discussion to make sure everyone can have their say.	The chairperson might not be that skilled at managing the discussion. They should receive training to help them develop this skill. This could be as simple as watching someone else chair a meeting to see how it is done.
Some agenda items were not discussed.	There were too many things to discuss.	Could some of the agenda items have been communicated in a different way? For instance, if an agenda item was simply to update people on a project, could attendees have had an email update instead?
		The chairperson could set time limits on discussions.
Decisions were not made.	The chairperson did not draw the discussion to a conclusion.	The chairperson needs to carefully direct the discussion so that if a decision is needed it can be made.
		The chairperson could hold a simple vote at the end of discussion on an agenda item.
People have not done the task they were allocated in the last meeting.	The minutes of the previous meeting were not sent out.	Make sure the minutes of a meeting are sent out to all attendees within a few days of the meeting. They will act as a reminder about what was discussed and what tasks where allocated to whom.
	The minutes are not clear.	Write the minutes as an accurate but easy to understand record of the meeting so that people know what is expected of them after the meeting. Use a simple format like the example in Figure 11.3.

Table 11.2: Problems that might occur in meetings

Chapter 11: Communication

MINI CASE STUDY

Valentina's awful meetings

Valentina leads a marketing team in Brasilia. She was upset when she overheard a member of staff saying they would rather clean their shared kitchen than attend another one of Valentina's meetings.

The problem was that, as team leader, Valentina often had lots of information to communicate with her team. Last week there had been 20 matters to discuss on the agenda, which they didn't get through because Mateo complained for a long time about not getting the minutes from a meeting two weeks ago. He used this as an excuse for not doing a job that he was meant to do. As well as chairing the meeting Valentina decided to take the minutes herself, because she did not want to listen to another ten-minute argument about whose turn it was to take the minutes, as happened at the last meeting.

After an hour only ten matters had been discussed and there was no time to deal with the other ten matters to be discussed. Of course, it didn't help that her administration assistant, Daniela, had not sent out some documents in advance so time was wasted in the meeting while people read them.

Questions:

1. Identify the problems that Valentina faced when preparing for and running her meeting.
2. Suggest three improvements that Valentina could make to her meetings so that they run more smoothly and are more effective in achieving the desired outcomes.

PROJECT PROMPT

Throughout your enterprise project you will need to have meetings to discuss different aspects of the project. Records of your meetings may be useful to you when writing up your project, and could be used as a source of evidence to support the things you are writing.

You can use the template at the end of this chapter to ensure you have successful meetings.

Presentations

One activity that often takes place at a meeting is a presentation. A presentation is a speech or talk that introduces a new idea or piece of work to an audience that makes use of the written, verbal and non-verbal communication skills of the presenter. Often presentations are supported by slides, handouts and visual aids.

Guidance for using slides in a presentation

- Write yourself a set of notes about what you are going to say and practise beforehand until you are confident.
- Only put short, key points or images on your slides that support what you are saying.
- Refer to key points or images on your slide but do not read out your slide. Assume your audience can read.

Guidance for using handouts in a presentation

- Decide if your handout is to be read during the presentation or afterwards.
- If it is to be read during the presentation, hand it out at the beginning, refer to it when you want your audience to read it and keep it short and simple so that it can be quickly read and not slow the flow of your presentation.
- If it is to be read after the presentation it can be handed out at the end and can be more detailed.
- Make sure the language and images used in handouts are the same as those used in your presentation and on slides if you have them.

Guidance for using visual aids in a presentation
- Decide if your visual aid needs to be viewed/handled during the presentation or afterwards.
- If you want it to be viewed/handled during the presentation, be aware that you may lose the concentration of your audience whilst they are viewing/handling the item.
- If you want it to be viewed/handled after the presentation make time for this and the potential questions it may raise.

PROJECT PROMPT

You will need to deliver an individual presentation as part of your project. Try to apply the tips described here so that you can demonstrate your written, verbal and non-verbal communication skills.

Formal report

A formal report is an official document created by an enterprise. Reports usually give an account of one matter based on thorough investigation, analysis and evaluation. Reports are often sent out with agendas for people to read prior to a meeting, and are usually supported by a presentation in the meeting. Although different enterprises may have particular ways of writing reports they all have the same general headings of title, introduction, findings, conclusions and recommendations, and appendices. Within each heading there are likely to be sub-headings, bullet points and links to appendix documents that contain further data such as tables and graphs.

The sections of a report

Title – in this section you need to put the date, who the report was written by, who it is written for, and the title of the report.

Introduction – the purpose of this section is to give the reader an idea of why the report was written and what they can expect to find in the report. There should be an explanation of why the report is being undertaken, a brief discussion of how research might take place, and some identification of the desired outcome.

Findings – the purpose of this section is to explain all the relevant data that has been found out from your primary and secondary research. Often writers create links from this section of the report to a document in the appendices to support the explanations.

Conclusions – the purpose of this section is to make decisions and recommendations. Often writers create links from this section of the report to a document in the appendices that supports the decision or recommendation that is being made.

a Analyse and interpret the data gathered through primary and secondary research. (What does it mean? Are findings as expected? What decisions or recommendations can be made based the analysis and interpretation?)

b Discuss how research went. (How well did research methods work? Are there problems with the information gathered? Are findings accurate and valid? Were there problems collecting your data and how were they overcome?)

c If your report was to be rewritten, would it be approached differently and how?

d Has any personal learning and development taken place due to undertaking this report?

Appendices – this is a where you would put all the documents that support the main report. Appendices should be carefully and logically ordered so that the reader can easily find an appendix that is referenced within the main report.

> **PROJECT PROMPT**
>
> In your project you will have to write two reports. By not writing in a report format you may limit the marks that you get. Remember, keep your communication formal, use headings, subheadings and bullet points, and make links to the appendix documents that support what you have written.

Chapter 11: Communication

Exam-style questions

Cora makes hand made pottery including bowls and plates which she sells at a local Saturday market. Demand for her products is high and Cora wants to start selling her pottery in a local shop. One of her friends knows a local shop keeper who may be willing to do so.

Cora will need to use formal communication to request a meeting. Cora knows if she can arrange a meeting with the shopkeeper verbal and non-verbal communication will be important if she is to be successful.

1. Define 'formal communication'. [2]
2. Explain two ways in which non-verbal communication can impact on what Cora says in the meeting. [6]
3. Explain why the language Cora uses in her meeting might be different to the language Cora might use with her friends. [6]
4. Referring to your enterprise project, evaluate how you used informal and formal communication to support the success of your enterprise. [15]
5. Describe one reason why an enterprise might hold a meeting. [2]
6. Refer back to the case study of Valentina's awful meetings. Valentina did not demonstrate the role of a chairperson well. Explain the role of a chairperson in a meeting. [4]
7. Referring to your enterprise project, evaluate how you used meetings, reports and presentations to support the success of your enterprise. [15]

Summary

You should know:

- that methods of communication can be formal or informal depending on the audience
- the appropriate types of communication to have with internal and external stakeholders
- how to plan for meetings
- the importance of meeting documents
- how to evaluate meetings and presentations.

Template 7: Planning and holding effective meetings

This template can be used to check that the key points have been covered when planning and holding meetings effectively.

Before the meeting
- Decide whether a meeting is needed
- Agree the purpose of the meeting
- Who needs to attend?
- How much time do you need?
- Identify a suitable date and time
- Find a suitable venue
- Let other people know about the meeting
- Prepare an agenda:
    - Review points from last meeting (if appropriate)
    - Ask people for agenda items
    - Make sure agenda is not too long
- Send attendees an invitation and copy of agenda.

During the meeting
- Introductions
- Agree who will chair the meeting, and who will take minutes
- Make a note of any apologies from people who cannot attend
- Review minutes from last meeting (if appropriate)
- Discuss each item on the agenda one at a time
- Ask if there are any additional issues to discuss
- Agree on who will be responsible for each action
- Agree a date and time for the next meeting (if necessary).

Chapter 11: Communication

After the meeting
- Evaluate the meeting:
    - Were all agenda items discussed?
    - Did the meeting run to time?
    - Were decisions taken?
    - Did everyone have an opportunity to contribute?
    - Were action points agreed and activities allocated?
- Send everyone a copy of the minutes (include people who could not attend).

Learning summary

In this chapter you will learn about:

- the formal sources of help and support for enterprise
- the informal sources of help and support for enterprise.

Chapter 12: Help and support for enterprise

Sources of help and support

There are various sources of help and support for upcoming and small organisations. Different sources of help and support are available in different contexts. The entrepreneur needs to consider the political and cultural environment of their enterprise. First, they must find out what is available in their country. Then, they need to identify appropriate sources of support for their particular enterprise.

Formal sources and the assistance they offer

Government/business agencies

The type of help given by the government varies from country to country. Here are some examples:

- **Government grants and loans.** A grant is a sum of money provided by the government to a business that does not have to be repaid. Grants can be offered for a range of reasons including supporting new enterprises when starting up, encouraging research and development and energy efficiency.
- **Subsidies.** A sum of money given by the government to businesses operating in certain industries to keep the prices of those goods/services low.
- **Setting up dedicated agencies.** Some governments create agencies to support and advise small enterprises. For example, the government of India created the National Small Industries Corporation Ltd (NSIC) to promote micro and small enterprises in the country.
- **Training.** Assistance to develop the skills and capability of staff is provided through apprenticeships. They are designed to provide work-based learning opportunities for young people. This enables companies to recruit labour more easily and at a lower cost.
- **Tax incentives.** Reduced tax rates or complete tax exemptions for some time are given to enterprises working in certain industries or located in certain areas. For example, in India, there are tax exemptions available for start-ups until 31 March 2019.

- **Relaxed government policies.** Policies like rapid and easy **business licensing**, encourage potential entrepreneurs to take the initiative to start their enterprise.

- **Special economic zones (SEZ).** This is an area in which business and trade laws are different from the rest of the country. The main aims of a SEZ are to increase trade and investment and create jobs by providing special economic policies, minimal **tariffs** and flexible governmental measures. For example, in the UAE, the government has created special 'free' zones with no foreign exchange controls or **trade barriers** and which have competitive **import duties**, financing costs, energy costs and real estate costs.

> **KEY TERMS**
>
> **Business licence:** A permit that allows a business to operate in a certain area and sell a specific product or service. It is issued by the government.
>
> **Tariff:** A tax/charge to be paid by a business to the government for importing (buying goods from other countries) and exporting (selling goods to other countries).
>
> **Trade barriers:** Steps taken by the government to control international trade. An example would be charging a tax on imports.
>
> **Import duties:** A tax to be paid by a business to the government for importing goods from another country.

MINI CASE STUDY

The Umm Al Moumineen Women's Association

The Umm Al Moumineen Women's Association was established in 1974 in Ajman, UAE, with the dual purpose of providing support to small enterprises managed by women and to preserve traditional activities as part of the country's cultural heritage. It operates a centre for continuous education for young married women to help them to finish their education, and also conducts workshops where women engage in traditional activities and receive a salary. It also provides dedicated support to women who are home-based entrepreneurs, by holding exhibitions that provide opportunities to market and sell their products. It conducts entrepreneurship training programmes and information sessions for women who have great ideas but lack the resources and initiative to start an enterprise, and provides information on how to gain start-up capital and market products.

Chapter 12: Help and support for enterprise

The association is funded by contributions from the ruler of Ajman and the Ministry of Labour, with revenues generated from activities such as fees for workshops, exhibitions and different types of training (e.g. computer skills, sewing, beautician, management and English).

Questions:
1. List the different ways in which The Umm Al Moumineen Women's Association offers support to women in the UAE.
2. Explain why you think women entrepreneurs in the UAE may need help and support to start an enterprise.
3. Why do you think the UAE government wants to promote women entrepreneurs?

Consultants

These are experts that specialise in all aspects of setting up and running an enterprise and charge a fee for providing their services. They have a good knowledge about the industry and legislation relevant to the enterprise and they can be hired for solving specific problems. For example, Tandem was founded in 2009 in Dubai, United Arab Emirates, and is dedicated to supporting start-ups and small businesses through every challenge they face by providing:

- business planning
- market research and analysis
- financial advice
- guidance, mentorship and advice.

> **TIP**
>
> Don't hesitate to contact people you think may have expert knowledge and who may be able to help you with your project.

Financial institutions

The amount of support provided can vary from country to country, but, generally, banks and institutions that provide micro finance can give ongoing advice and access to financial services to businesses and individual households. Financial institutions can provide support to small businesses by providing start-up loans, **micro loans** (small amounts of money can be borrowed more easily than by a

> **KEY TERM**
>
> **Micro loans:** Small amounts of money that can be borrowed more easily than by a traditional bank loan.

traditional bank loan) and asset loans (borrowing money against an asset that you own). Financial institutions not only provide start-up loans but also loans for continuous operation.

> **KEY TERM**
>
> **Seed capital:** The money needed to start a business. This money often comes from the owner's personal assets and their friends and family.

Charities and not-for-profit organisations

These are organisations that raise funds by donations and direct them towards a social cause. They raise these funds by their own entrepreneurial activities, mobilising funds from corporations and foundations and gathering gifts and contributions. For example, Trickle Up is a not-for-profit international development organisation that provides the very poorest people with **seed capital** grants, skills training and coaching, and the support they need to create small businesses.

Teachers

Entrepreneurship education is on the rise, both at school and university level. The role of teachers is vital in providing theoretical and practical learning opportunities to enable students to turn ideas into action.

Teachers are there to guide and support you throughout the enterprise project from planning through to implementation.

MINI CASE STUDY

Peter's Party Favours

NFTE is the Network for Teaching Entrepreneurship. It is an international, non-profit charitable organisation which introduces low-income teenagers to entrepreneurship, teaching them to develop and run their own small businesses.

NFTE enables young people to develop the skills and understanding to make a success of their lives. At 18, Omayra Rodriguez Matthews had a one-year old son, Peter. Omayra set up a business called Peter's Party Favours, making Latin American party gifts (called *capias*), table centrepieces and fridge magnets. Omayra joined the entrepreneurship course and learnt how to turn a hobby and passion into a money-making venture.

Chapter 12: Help and support for enterprise

Questions:

1. Using examples from this case, explain the importance of training programmes and entrepreneurial education in promoting upcoming and small enterprises.
2. What challenges would Omayra have faced if he had not had any education/ training on enterprise skills?

> **TIP**
>
> If you are unable to use the internet to do the research for your project, your teacher may be able to guide you to other sources of information, such as business journals, local trade magazines and organisations that you may be able to use.

Business networks

Business networking events organised locally or on a larger scale bring together people from different experience levels and backgrounds. Business networking helps bring together people looking for sharing and developing their ideas, inspiration, advice, opportunities and **mentors**. These events are not only inspiring, they are also great opportunities for meeting potential investors and business partners.

> **KEY TERMS**
>
> **Business network:** A group of likeminded people/ entrepreneurs who meet on a regular basis to share ideas and explore future business partnerships.
>
> **Mentor:** An expert/ experienced person who agrees to provide dedicated advice and support.

Other entrepreneurs

Meeting with other entrepreneurs, either through business networks or individually, provides an exceptional opportunity to share ideas, learn from each other and possibly form business partnerships. An experienced entrepreneur may even be able to act as a mentor and provide dedicated advice and support.

> **ACTIVITY 12.1**
>
> Working in a pair or a group, use the internet, business journals or other sources of information to find out what kind of support is offered by businesses and business networks in your area.

Informal sources and the assistance they offer

Friends and family

Friends and family members can inspire and encourage a young entrepreneur to keep going when things are not going as expected and can provide support in times of challenges. Family and friends are often the first people that entrepreneurs turn to when they need to raise seed/initial capital for their new enterprise.

There are, however, possible drawbacks to taking help from friends and family. There may be undue influence by some individuals, which may lead to decisions based on emotion rather than reason. Arrangements for sharing responsibility may be informal or unclear, and may cause disagreements or inefficient working. There may also be personal consequences of getting into debt with friends and family.

> **TIP**
>
> Your friends studying the same subject as you in your school or elsewhere may be a valuable source of support, advice and information.

Suitability of different sources of help and support

The suitability of different sources of help and support depends on the nature of the business and the type of support needed. For example, someone wanting to start a hairdressing business might rely on informal sources of support like friends and family for advice, emotional support and initial capital. They could also use formal sources of support like networking with similar businesses to exchange ideas, government agencies to understand all the required legislation and financial institutions to gain start-up loans.

> **TIP**
>
> Don't forget to use your personal network (people you may know at school and outside) to help you with the research, planning and implementation of your project.

MINI CASE STUDY

Help and support for entrepreneurs

Read the following range of forms of help and support that are available to entrepreneurs around the world.

Youth network

The ASEANpreneurs is a youth-run organisation managed by the Entrepreneurship Society of the National University of Singapore and students from partner universities. Its main aim is to inspire youth and encourage entrepreneurship in the ASEAN region (consisting of Indonesia, Malaysia, the Philippines, Singapore and Thailand). It organises regular events to bring together aspiring entrepreneurs and business leaders to promote the sharing and discussion of business ideas, gain guidance and possibly meet potential business partners.

Mentoring programme

Mowgli Mentoring is a not-for-profit organisation that provides mentors to potential and new entrepreneurs. It offers mentoring support to upcoming entrepreneurs by bringing together groups of mentors and entrepreneurs for an initial training session to build relationships, match them together in one-to-one pairs and then follow it up with online support for a year. Mowgli Mentoring has so far launched 20 Programs in Jordan, Lebanon, Syria and the UK and provided volunteer mentors to 153 entrepreneurs across these countries.

Start-up funding support

Ruwad Establishment in the UAE provides start-up funding in the form of an interest-free loan (up to AED 300 000), or in the form of a bank loan that Ruwad Establishment helps to arrange/negotiate with an Islamic bank (up to AED 1 million).

Casual Networking

MAKE business hub is a café in the heart of Dubai, offering various communal work spaces, private meeting rooms, charging stations and presentation equipment. It makes working easy for Dubai's self-employed, start-up entrepreneurs and professionals on the go. Most importantly it provides a great networking opportunity for individuals to meet and form connections.

Social media networking

Youth Entrepreneurial Network Malaysia is an online resource and community for entrepreneurs. It aims to bring together the young entrepreneurs in Malaysia by initiating and supporting entrepreneurship and business conferences for experienced and young entrepreneurs.

TV media

Dragons' Den is a series of reality television shows, where potential entrepreneurs pitch their business ideas to a panel of venture capitalists in order to secure investment from them. Its main aim is to encourage entrepreneurship and small businesses. The original Dragons' Den started in Japan but is now broadcast in 23 countries.

Questions:

1. How do you think programmes like Dragons' Den help support small enterprises?
2. Explain which means of networking – youth, social media or casual, as mentioned here – you think is the most effective.
3. Explain how the different mechanisms of help and support mentioned here help aspiring and upcoming entrepreneurs.

PROJECT PROMPT

It isn't a requirement for the coursework, but it would still be useful to research what sort of help and support your enterprise could get from the government of your country.

Are there any not-for-profit organisations or charities that correspond with the vision and cause of your enterprise, and which may be able to provide support to your enterprise?

What practical help and support can you get from your family and friends?

Chapter 12: Help and support for enterprise

Exam-style questions

1. State **two** ways in which financial institutions can provide support to small enterprises. [2]
2. Identify and explain **two** ways in which friends and family can provide help and support to an enterprise. [4]
3. Referring to the case study above, explain **two** ways in which the MAKE business hub café in Dubai helps upcoming entrepreneurs. [6]
4. Using examples, explain **three** different ways the government can provide help and support to enterprises. [6]
5. Evaluate which is the best source of help and support to your enterprise. Justify your recommendation. [10]

Summary

You should know:

- grants, subsidies and tax reliefs are some ways in which the government provides help and support to enterprises
- friends and family are often the first people entrepreneurs turn to for seed capital. Though they can provide the encouragement that is needed in challenging times, there may be undue influence by certain overpowering individuals causing disagreements and inefficiencies.
- enterprises may use both formal and informal sources of help and support. The choice of formal support they use depends on their need and the nature of their business.

158

Chapter 13
Evaluation

Learning summary

In this chapter you will learn about:

- the principles of analysis and evaluation
- how to evaluate the finances of your project
- how to evaluate communications within your project.

Introduction

In your exam and project you need to be able to show analysis and evaluation skills. This means you must do more than present information, such as stating what you did or quoting results from market research.

Analysis involves selecting, explaining or interpreting information to help break down an issue into smaller parts.

Evaluation requires you to make a judgement or decision based on evidence presented and reasoned explanations.

Making a decision or choice is not evaluation. It is the reasoning *behind* the decision that matters. Evaluation is subjective. Two people with the same information can reach a different conclusion. That's fine. What is important is being able to clearly explain how and why you made your choice, and why you think it is better than possible alternatives.

It is important not to jump to conclusions without considering all relevant information first. Effective analysis and evaluation rely on you thinking clearly about issues, understanding the links between ideas and using information in a logical way to help answer the problem or question set.

This can involve:

- identifying and considering the advantages and disadvantages of other points of view and different options
- understanding the implications and effect of different actions and ideas
- questioning ideas, for example by identifying mistakes and weaknesses in points made
- being able to build an argument
- identifying which information is relevant and important
- looking for evidence to support points made
- making informed decisions.

You already do many of these activities without thinking about it, when making everyday decisions, such as what to do or buy.

For the exam, you need to be able to show the reasons behind your thinking in a structured way to show how you reached your decision.

Chapter 13: Evaluation

> **TIP**
>
> When a question asks you to consider different options or ideas, do not simply list the advantages and disadvantages. This is knowledge. You must try to apply the information to the scenario (or project) and explain why each point is relevant and should be considered.

Ways to develop analysis and evaluation skills

There are many techniques and methods to help you develop the skills needed in analysis and evaluation. For example, problem-solving, critical thinking and decision-making activities provide plenty of opportunities for you to identify links between ideas and consider different solutions. Debates are also a good way to discuss different points of view and learn how to build an argument.

A good way to start any analysis is with five simple questions — **who? what? where? when?** and **why?** The answers can help you gather information to solve the problem or guide you towards finding the relevant information you need.

> **ACTIVITY 13.1**
>
> Think of something that someone has recently told you. It could be anything from a news story to information about something happening at home or school.
>
> Ask yourself the following questions:
>
> - Who said it?
> - What did they say?
> - Where did they say it?
> - When did they say it?
> - Why did they say it?
>
> Do the answers to these questions change how you view the information? Did it matter who told you the information or where or when you were told? Do you need to gather more information, or are you happy to accept what has been said?

Ideas and arguments should be based on accurate and reliable information so it is important that you do not simply accept what you are told. If not, it can lead to the wrong decisions being made.

Always try to check sources to make sure you can trust information. You need to know if the information is up-to-date, and be aware of any bias.

When analysing an issue, keep asking yourself *how* and *why*. This will help you to look at things in detail and deepen your understanding.

For example, new enterprises are at greater risk of failing.

- Why? Because they lack finance.
- Why? Because banks are reluctant to lend.
- Why? Because new enterprises have less security to offer so are seen as high risk.

ACTIVITY 13.2

Repeat the 'why' analysis for other possible reasons why new enterprises are at greater risk of failing. For example, lack of enterprise experience. For each reason, try to find at least three 'whys'.

You can use the how or why approach with other statements to help you practise and develop your analysis skills.

TIP

Remember, when looking for answers, think:

- What?
- When?
- Where?
- How?
- Why?

Considering different options

You will often need to explore an issue in more detail by breaking it down into smaller parts. To do this, all relevant factors or ideas need to be considered before making a decision. This can help reduce the risk of mistakes or wrong actions taken.

Writing a list of advantages and disadvantages is one way to identify ideas or different points of view that you can then explore.

For example:

Factor or issue 1:	Advantages/pros	Disadvantages/cons
Factor or issue 2:	Advantages/pros	Disadvantages/cons
Factor or issue 3:	Advantages/pros	Disadvantages/cons

You may need to add more boxes, depending on the number of points identified.

ACTIVITY 13.3

The government of Country A plans to build a new airport to cope with the increase in business and tourist passengers. Most businesses, including holiday companies, support this plan. However, the local community and environmental groups do not want the new airport to be built.

What factors should be involved in the final decision?

Identify the relevant factors that need to be considered in this scenario, using a grid similar to the example above.

By identifying relevant factors, you can then begin to consider which ones are important. One way to do this is by looking at the possible effects of each factor. For example, if you identify something as an advantage, why or how is this advantage created and what is the impact of it on the decision?

Developing depth to your analysis

In order to show good or excellent analysis, you need to develop points made. You must try to avoid jumping to the end point without explaining how you got there.

Sample answer:

> Manisha was pleased with the results as she made extra revenue.

This is a basic analysis as it only explains the final outcome. This statement needs to be developed to show *how* or *why* she was able to achieve the extra revenue.

To add depth you need to discuss the implications of points made. To help you do this, try to use connecting words to develop points. A simple and easy method to use is **BLT – 'because', 'leads to' and 'therefore'**. Using connecting words, such as BLT or others, such as 'as a result', 'so' or 'this means' will help you to think about *why* something happens, *what* the result of it is and *how* it affects the enterprise.

For example:

> Manisha was pleased with the results as she made extra revenue. This is **because** she chose a suitable method of communication **leading** to more of her potential target market being aware of her phone cases. **Therefore**, she was able to increase the number of sales she made.

Role of evidence

When trying to build an argument or question ideas, a good question to ask is 'How do you know?'

Evidence is important as it provides the proof to support points being made. Use evidence to help build your argument. For the case study, use the information from the text. Likewise, for your enterprise project, you can use information including customer feedback, sales or financial data as evidence. All evidence used needs to be clearly referenced so make sure you specify numbers or quote customer comments rather than simply say 'My research showed this'.

Think Point, evidence, explanation

Look at the following example:

> **Olivia's jam enterprise**
>
> Because of a delay in starting, Olivia did no market research. This meant that she did not anticipate the demand for her product so she struggled to meet orders on time. This meant that she lost some customers, who then told others about her poor level of service and discouraged them from buying her products.

This explanation demonstrates good analysis, but there is little evidence to support the points being made.

ACTIVITY 13.4

Identify the evidence used to support this explanation.
Identify ways in which more evidence could be included.

Evaluation

An evaluation should consist of two main parts: the what (judgement) and the why (justification).

- Having considered different options you will have to make decisions in order to select the best option, so state **what** you think should happen.
- Any decision must be supported by reasons and evidence so the second thing to explain is **why**? Why did you choose this option and why is it better than the alternative?

To do this you must have discussed the benefits, disadvantages and potential effects of each option. In simple terms, you have to analyse before you can evaluate.

In your evaluation, focus on the factor or points you consider to be most important.

Using a set of criteria can help you assess the value of different options or ideas. This can help you rank different factors or ideas. For example, when selecting your source of finance, factors such as 'purpose', 'amount needed' and 'cost of finance' can help you rank different options.

ACTIVITY 13.5

You have been asked to advise a family friend about which is the best mobile phone to buy.
Create a set of criteria you could use to help you make your decision. Which factor do you think is the most important? Based on your criteria, which do you think is the best mobile phone to buy?

An evaluation should always be based on previous points or arguments made. However, do not simply repeat what you have already written. Instead, try to expand on previous analysis to show how or why your argument proves you have made a suitable choice.

MINI CASE STUDY

Caleb's candles

Caleb studied enterprise at school. After leaving school he plans to start up a small enterprise making candles. Caleb likes the idea of being a sole trader business so that he can make his own decisions. Caleb has used most of his savings on developing his product. His market research was very successful with four shops wanting to place regular orders for his candles. Caleb has worked out he needs $100 to buy more materials and start his enterprise.

His friend, Leanne, works in a gift shop. She has suggested becoming his business partner. For a 50:50 share of the profits, she would be willing to provide the finance needed and help with marketing.

Evaluate whether a partnership is the most appropriate type of business organisation for Caleb's enterprise. Justify your recommendation.

Sample evaluation

I think the lack of finance is the most important factor stopping his success. He has already used most of his savings developing his candles so he has to find another source of finance to buy the materials he needs. While he could ask the bank for a loan, there is no guarantee they would agree to this, especially as his is a new enterprise. If they do, he would have to pay additional interest, which would increase his costs. As the other person is his friend there is less risk of disagreements. She can also add experience as she has worked in a gift shop so may be able to suggest ways to attract more customers, which could lead to more sales and possibly a larger amount of profit than he could make on his own. Added to this, the fact that she has the finance available would allow him to be able to obtain the materials he needs. With a partner, Caleb would have to share profits, which would reduce the amount he receives. However, without money to make his candles he would not be able to make a profit anyway. So for these reasons I think a partnership is the best option.

ACTIVITY 13.6

Write an evaluation to support the idea that Caleb should set up the enterprise as a sole trader business.

Chapter 13: Evaluation

Evaluating the project

This is a reflective activity in which you are required to evaluate how well your project was implemented. In simple terms, what went well and why? What didn't go well, and why? You need to be honest. What were your objectives? Remember, it does not matter if your project made any money or not. The project is a learning opportunity, so focus on what you learnt during the process, rather than the final outcome.

Remember, even if you completed your project as part of a group, each individual should write their own report.

There is a word limit so it is important to try to be clear and concise when writing and focus only on the areas required.

The only skills being assessed in this task are analysis and evaluation. Do not simply describe the activities you did.

For each option chosen, you will be expected to:

- analyse and evaluate both positive and negative outcomes for each aspect of your enterprise
- use evidence gathered as part of the project to support the points you make as part of your analysis and evaluation of the financial aspects of your enterprise
- give clear and reasoned recommendations for improvements.

> **TIP**
>
> When planning your report, always try to think 'why?' and then write down your answer. Keep repeating this process until it reaches a clear outcome.
>
> Be selective in the points that you discuss. Try to avoid simple statements, such as 'This was successful', without explaining why you think this was the case. You need to be able to provide clear reasons to support your point of view.

> **ACTIVITY 13.7**
>
> Identify what is wrong with this extract.
> Suggest ways in which it could be improved.
>
> *Planning and Implementation*
> *We planned what we were going to do in a detailed action plan and diary containing what we were going to do. We were very careful to follow each step,*

as these steps were the difference between us failing or being successful. Our finance part went well. Our products had to be sold for different prices than what we had planned and this did cause us problems.

We raised money by fundraising, and kept a note of everything in our diary. This was a good idea. The fundraising helped us attract attention that helped us be successful. We did have problems with our planning, and if I were to do this again I would definitely have a more detailed action plan.

Wherever possible, provide evidence to support what you are saying. You may find it helpful to keep a journal to record what happened and when, any feedback received, as well as your thoughts and observations.

It is the depth and quality of analysis and evaluation that is important rather than the number of points made. Avoid writing generic lists of advantages and disadvantages. Focus on the main points and explain, in turn, why or how they are relevant to your project. Try to link together and build upon each point to show how or why something is important and the effect it has on your enterprise. Remember to use connecting words to help you develop points.

PROJECT PROMPT

For each point, explain what the issue was, why it was important, whether it could be seen as a success or a failure and explain how this issue affected your enterprise. At each stage, try to use evidence to support what you are saying.

When writing up your conclusions, include a summary of any important findings you identified from carrying out your project.

Recommendations should focus on improvements associated with issues identified in your report. If you were to do the project again, what would you do differently and why?

Keep the recommendations focused on the two areas discussed in the report. For example, if you select internal communication, there is no need to make any recommendations about marketing communication or finance.

Chapter 13: Evaluation

Possible issues for discussion

The following list of prompts is not exhaustive and may not cover all or any of the issues faced by your enterprise project. The issues you discuss and their impact will depend entirely on what happened in your project. Each issue could have positive or negative effects for your enterprise.

Planning and Implementation

In your project, you *must* evaluate planning and implementation as this is a compulsory element. There are plenty of issues that you could discuss under this heading, but you only need to discuss the issues that had a significant effect on your project.

Planning

Your action plan will have been prepared *before* the project started so it is highly likely that it will need to be amended at some stage. This is because, however well you try to plan, unforeseen things can happen, such as power cuts, changes in the weather or a supplier unexpectedly runs out of inventory. So, keep a note of any changes as this can provide topics and evidence that you can use in your report. It can also be used as evidence for Paper 1 as some exam questions will relate to your project.

The following prompts may help you to evaluate your planning and implementation.

Implementation

- How well were you able to put the plan into action?
- What methods did you use to plan the project? How well did they work?
- In your project, you identified two or three key risks. Were the actions to manage these risks successful?
- Did anything happen to change your plans? Could or should you have expected these issues?
- Did you have to change what you planned to sell? Why was this? For example, did one of your competitors change what it planned to sell?
- Did you keep your action plan up-to-date?
- How effective was the monitoring?

- Were there any differences between predictions made in planning and actual events? How did this affect your enterprise?
- Were there any unexpected issues or events that affected your enterprise?
- Were supplies available on time? If not, what effect did this have on your project timings?
- Was the equipment available?
- How effective was the pricing method used? Did you change your pricing during the project? Why?
- Did you select a suitable location? Would you change your location if you did the project again?
- Did anything happen that made you change what and when you sold your products?
- How effective was your planning?
- If you were to repeat the project would you change anything?

Market research

- Was your market research helpful?
- How reliable and relevant was your market research?
- If you had more time, would you use the same method of market research again? What additional information would have been helpful to collect?
- Did you come across any problems with the data collection?
- Was there any particular part of your research that affected your decisions or choice of project?

You may want to include extracts of your market research as evidence to support the points made. For example, a question that did not gather the information you wanted due to how it was worded.

> **PROJECT PROMPT**
>
> You may find there are many things you could comment on that happen during your project. Remember, the depth of analysis and evaluation is key to accessing the higher mark bands. There is also a word limit so make what you write count. Focus on two or three significant issues for each area as the basis for discussion.

Chapter 13: Evaluation

Ideally, your report should cover both positive and negative aspects; as with any project not everything is likely to go to plan.

For example, Gabriel and Kemar decided to sell ice cream at a school event for their enterprise project.

> On the day of the sale, the fridge didn't work and the ice cream melted. This created a problem. Fortunately, Kemar had the idea to use the ice cream to make smoothies. This placed our business in competition with others so we had to work hard to create sales.

If writing about this issue in the report, areas for discussion may include:

- Why didn't the fridge work? If the fridge was old, could or should this problem have been anticipated? If so, how does this reflect on the effectiveness of the planning?
- What exactly was the problem caused by the lack of a fridge?
- What was the possible impact on the enterprise if they had not had the idea to make smoothies?
- Explain how switching to smoothies altered their plans, and its effect on what had to be done on the day and the impact on your project.
- If they were to do the project again, would they sell ice cream or smoothies? Why?

Optional areas

You have a choice for the second aspect. Make sure the aspect you select is appropriate for your project based on the issues faced and size of group.

Sources of finance

In the planning phase of your enterprise you will have researched and decided upon the most appropriate source of finance for your situation. Sometimes, getting your chosen source of finance goes smoothly, but sometimes you need to think of an alternative. Occasionally, your chosen source of finance turns out to be the wrong one and you would have been better off going for another source.

If you obtained your chosen source of finance:

- Was it easy to get?
- Did you get as much as you wanted? If not, how did you make up the shortfall?

If you didn't get your chosen source of finance:

- Why not? Is there anything you could have done better to improve your chances of getting your chosen source of finance?
- What source of finance did you end up getting and how well did that work?

If you were to run the enterprise again would you choose the same source of finance or a different one?

> **PROJECT PROMPT**
>
> Make sure that you refer to evidence to support points made. For example, if you had to negotiate for your finance you could provide evidence of that negotiation in the appendix.

Cash flow forecast

You may have created a cash flow forecast to predict cash inflows and outflows of your enterprise whilst it was operating. Your cash flow forecast will have been based on estimates for income and expenditure and whilst these may have proven quite similar to the real income and expenditure they are unlikely to be identical.

To analyse the differences between what you forecasted and the actual flow of cash in to and out of your enterprise, you should create a new cash flow which uses the actual figures. This will allow you to:

- investigate the similarities and differences between your predicted figures and the actual figures
- explain key differences and the impact they had on the running of your enterprise. Remember to give both positive and negative.
- suggest how you would try to improve your forecasting if you were to run this enterprise again so that you build on the positives and reduce negative impacts.

Chapter 13: Evaluation

> **PROJECT PROMPT**
>
> You could refer to the original cash flow forecast that you created as evidence. If you do so, don't forget to include the actual cash flow that you created in the appendix and also refer this.

Break-even

You may have calculated break-even point as part of the planning. This figure will have been based upon estimates you made about your enterprise's revenue, costs and what price you would charge for your product. The actual figures may be different.

To analyse the differences between what you predicted as your break-even point and the actual break-even point, you need to calculate a new break-even point which uses the actual figures of your enterprise. This will allow you to:

- investigate the similarities and differences between your predicted break-even point and the actual break-even point
- explain the impact of differences in break-even point on your enterprise
- suggest how you could improve the break-even point of your enterprise if you were to run it again.

> **PROJECT PROMPT**
>
> When evaluating your project, make sure you refer to evidence to support the points made in your project. For example, you could refer back to your original calculation of break-even. If so, include your calculation in the appendix.

Income statement

Now that you have run your enterprise for a set period of time you will have your actual financial figures and can produce an income statement. This will allow you to:

- give the gross profit and net profit for your enterprise
- investigate and explain the differences between the gross profit and profit of your enterprise
- suggest ways in which you could improve the profit of your enterprise if you were to run the enterprise again.

PROJECT PROMPT

Make sure that you refer to the evidence when writing about the income statement. Place the income statement in the appendix and refer to it.

ACTIVITY 13.8

Franco ran a car wash at his school for his enterprise project. This is an extract from his project report in which he wrote about the finances of his enterprise. He thought it was a really good evaluation of his finances but his teacher told him it wasn't a very strong answer. Read through the extract and write some advice for Franco on how to improve his analysis and evaluation.

When planning Franco's Car Wash one of the things I did was create simple prediction of income and expenditure (Appendix 1). I expected a total income of $80, of which $20 was from my own savings to pay for the start-up costs of my enterprise project. The other $60 was my prediction for how much revenue I would get from selling my services. I researched the costs of the things that I needed to buy to make my enterprise work and this came to $35.60. This meant I had a predicted profit of $44.40

After 2 days of washing cars I produced a record of my actual income and expenditure (Appendix 2). This shows that my expenditure was more than I predicted at $59.60. Fortunately I also had predicted sales income of $80. I invested $20 of my own money to start up the car wash. Some of the things I needed to buy were more expensive than I expected so I agreed with the school that I would pay for the car park space and water out of my profits. Once I paid myself back the $20 I invested there was $40.40 left, which I donated to charity.

Chapter 13: Evaluation

Appendix 1 – Predicted income and expenditure

Item	Income ($)	Expenditure ($)
Investment from savings	20	
Sales revenue	60	
Total income	80	
Rent of car park space		10
Contribution to school water		10
Buckets		6
Car shampoo		4.75
Sponges		2.85
Drying cloths		2
Total expenditure		35.60
Profit/Loss	44.40	

Appendix 2 – Actual income and expenditure

Item	Income ($)	Expenditure ($)
Investment from savings	20	
Sales revenue	80	
Total income	100	
Rent of car park space		10
Contribution to school water		10
Buckets		8
Car shampoo		4.75
Sponges		2.85
Drying cloths		4
Repayment of investment		20
Total expenditure		59.60
Profit/Loss	40.40	

Marketing communication

In your project you may have discussed possible methods of marketing communication you planned to use to attract customers to your enterprise.

The focus of this section of your report should be to look at how effective were your chosen methods of marketing communication.

It is important to remember that you should only discuss marketing communications in this section. If you wish to discuss other elements of the marketing mix or market research, these should be included in the planning and implementation section of your report.

PROJECT PROMPT

If choosing this option, do not repeat your explanations behind your choice of marketing communication. Focus on writing about how effective the actual marketing communications selected were. Remember, it is perfectly acceptable to say that the chosen methods were not successful and explain why they did not work, and the implications of this for your project.

The following prompts may help you to evaluate the methods you used for marketing communication.

For each of your chosen methods of marketing communication:

- Did your potential customers notice the method you used?
- Did the method help attract customers to buy your products or services? Why?
- Do you think it was a suitable method to use, and why? If so, explain the effect on your enterprise. Can you explain possible reasons why they worked?
- If the method did not work, what was the effect on your enterprise? Can you explain possible reasons why it did not work as expected? How did you attract customers to your enterprise?
- As part of your planning you may have estimated the number of customers you expected to get. Did you get the number of customers you expected? If you received more or fewer customers, why do you think this was the case, and how did it impact what you did?

Chapter 13: Evaluation

- Suggest ways in which you could improve the marketing communications you used if you were to run the enterprise again.
- Would you still use the same methods again? Why? If not, which methods would you choose?

You may have used more than one method of marketing communication. If so, which one was most effective? Why do you think this?

Did you change from the planned methods identified when you planned your project?

- If so, why did you change?
- What method of marketing communication did you end up using, and how well did that work?
- If you were to run the enterprise again, would you choose the same methods of marketing communication or different ones? Explain why.

> **PROJECT PROMPT**
>
> In your project make sure you refer to evidence to support points made. For marketing communications, this could be forecast and actual sales data to show the level of customers and sales, feedback from the original questionnaires created when you were choosing your project and/or results of customer satisfaction surveys used when selling or customer comments.

MINI CASE STUDY

P&N's Pens

Natalia and Paolo planned to sell stationery for their project.

The poster was more effective than using social media. Everyone who came to our stall said they knew about us from seeing the posters around school. Having obtained permission to use the school notice boards was helpful. This meant few posters were torn down which increased the potential number of people seeing them, and therefore lead to more people visiting our stall.

Another positive about the posters was people liked them. One of the comments on our feedback sheet said 'Simple, fun poster – I wanted to see what the offers were'. They liked the posters because they were easy to read and clearly explained what we were selling. Because the posters attracted lots of people, this meant we didn't have to spend money on any other marketing which meant that we could afford to buy more stationery and offer the choices and great prices that we had promised our customers.

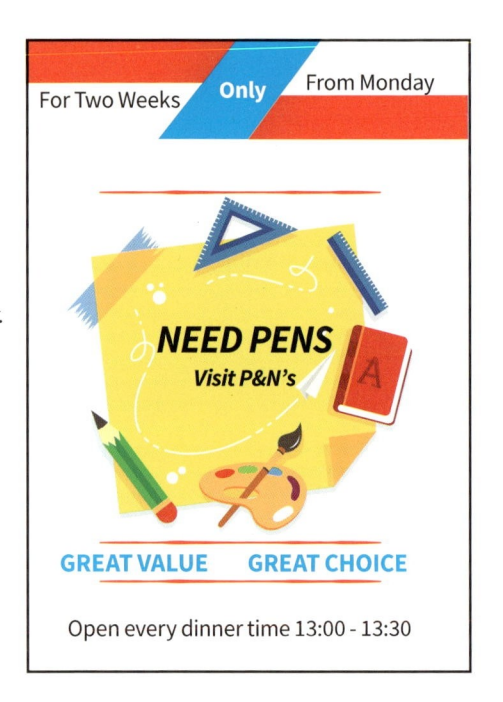

> For Two Weeks   Only   From Monday
>
> **NEED PENS**
> Visit P&N's
>
> **GREAT VALUE   GREAT CHOICE**
>
> Open every dinner time 13:00 - 13:30

Internal communications

Good communication is important for any enterprise. When organising and carrying out your project you will have needed to keep in touch with others in your group. How did you do this, and how successful were the methods that you decided to use?

> **TIP**
>
> Remember that you can only select this option if you were involved in a group project.

Do not confuse the methods of communication used with other stakeholders, such as suppliers, lenders or customers, as this is not what the question is about.

As with the other optional areas, there is no need to explain why you selected the methods. Instead focus on whether they were suitable choices for your group to use.

Chapter 13: Evaluation

The following prompts may help you to evaluate the methods you used for internal communication.

Meetings

A group meeting should have been arranged to discuss ideas, or as part of your planning and implementation for your project.

For these meetings:

- Did you have an agenda? If so, was it helpful, and if so, how and why? If not, do you think an agenda would have been useful?
- Do you think the meetings were well organised? Why? For example, was someone put in charge of the meetings? Did they take place when arranged and did they run to time?
- Were minutes taken, and were these accurately recorded? If not, did this cause any problems, and how did this affect the project?
- Were suitable actions agreed during the meetings? Were the actions given to specific team members? Was the method used to distribute the minutes a suitable choice? Why?
- What plans were put in place to monitor the agreed actions? How effective were these methods?
- Was having meetings helpful for the project? Why? If not, can you explain possible reasons why they did not work as expected?
- Suggest ways in which you could improve how the meetings were arranged and managed if you were to run the enterprise again.
- If you were to do the project again, would you use meetings? Why? If not, why and which methods would you choose?

For each of your chosen methods for internal communication, you need to decide how effective the method was. For example:

- Do you think it was a suitable method to use, and why?
- Did all members of the team use the methods chosen? If so, how effective were they? If not, why not?
- Did the methods work as well as you had hoped or planned? Why?
- Would you use this method again? Why? If not, why not, and which methods would you choose?

- You may have used more than one method for your internal communication. If so, which one was most effective? Why do you think this?
- Did you change from the methods you planned to use? If so, why did you change?
- What method of internal communication did you end up using, and how well did that work?
- If you were to run the enterprise again, would you choose the same methods of internal communication or different ones?

> **PROJECT PROMPT**
>
> Make sure you refer to evidence to support points made. For internal communication, this could be a copy of the minutes used as part of the meeting and/or examples of messages sent between team members. These could be included in the appendix and referred to in the report or featured as a short extract placed in the report itself.

> **ACTIVITY 13.9**
>
> Hal, Alex, Jane and Amy's group decided to sell t-shirts for their enterprise project. To help her write her report for her project, Amy kept a diary. An extract of this is shown here:
>
> | Issue | What happened? |
> |---|---|
> | Discussion at meeting | For the first meeting, there was no agenda although we had lots of things to sort out before we did the market research. No one seemed to be in charge. We all spent ages talking but no clear decisions seemed to be made. Minutes taken in meeting were sent to everyone by email but people disagreed about what was said. |
>
> Imagine you are Amy. Use this information to write a possible evaluation of the meeting issue. What recommendations would you suggest to improve how the meetings were organised?

Chapter 13: Evaluation

Checklist

1. Consider both the strengths and weaknesses of each aspect.
2. You do not need to discuss every issue. Focus on three (and a maximum of four) key issues for each area.
3. For each issue, explain clearly what the issue is and its effect on your enterprise.
4. Present your analysis and evaluation clearly and concisely. Remember to develop each point made to show the implications for your project.
5. Use evidence to support all points made.
6. Recommendations should be linked to the areas selected and should focus on possible improvements or actions.

Summary

Enterprise is a skill-based subject so knowledge alone is not enough to do well. You will be expected to show a range of skills, including analysis and evaluation. These skills can be developed and improved with time so practice is important.

You should know:

- how to show a range of skills, including analysis and evaluation.

Action plan: A list of tasks that need to be completed in order for a set goal to be achieved.

Aim: An overall goal that an enterprise wants to achieve.

Analyse: Examine in detail to show meaning, identify elements and the relationship between them.

Apologies: An item on the minutes of a meeting which shows the people who were invited to attend, but unable to do so.

Assets: Objects that are owned by the business.

Audience: The organisation/ group/individual that you are communicating with.

Break-even point: The point at which income from sales will cover all the enterprise's costs.

Business Enterprise: An organisation that has profit as its main aim.

Business licence: A permit that allows a business to operate in a certain area and sell a specific product or service. It is issued by the government.

Business network: A group of likeminded people/entrepreneurs who meet on a regular basis to share ideas and explore future business partnerships.

Business plan: A formal document that gives the aims of the enterprise and outlines ways those aims will be achieved.

Cash flow: The movement of money in and out of the enterprise.

Cash inflow: Any cash that comes into the enterprise.

Cash outflow: Any cash that goes out of the enterprise.

Co-operative: A type of business organisation that is owned and managed by people who use its services or who work there.

Contribution: Part of the calculation to work out break-even point:
Contribution per unit = variable costs per unit – sale price per unit.

Cost of sales: The costs that are directly linked to generating sales, such as raw materials and the labour of those directly involved in production.

Cost: Cash that an enterprise spends to produce its goods or services.

Customer retention: Measuring how loyal customers are to an enterprise (and the likelihood of them buying its products or services again).

Customer satisfaction: The extent to which customers are pleased with the products and services provided by an enterprise.

Glossary

Customer: A person or organisation that buys goods/materials or services from an enterprise.

Deficit: On a cash flow forecast, if the cash that comes into the enterprise is less than the cash that goes out, then there is a deficit of cash.

Define: Give precise meaning.

Describe: State the points of a topic/give characteristics and main features.

Discuss: Write about issue(s) or topic(s) in depth in a structured way.

Enterprise process: The various stages involved in starting and running an enterprise.

Enterprise: An organisation or business managed by one or more individuals who are able to take the initiative to make decisions and take calculated risks.

Entrepreneur: A person who starts up a new business or enterprise.

Ethics: Moral values and principles that govern a person's behaviour or the conducting of an activity.

Evaluate: Judge or calculate the quality, importance, amount, or value of something.

Expenditure: All the money that goes out of an enterprise.

Explain: Set out purposes or reasons/make the relationships between things evident/provide why and/or how and support with relevant evidence.

External sources of finance: Money that is found outside the enterprise.

Finance: The activities of an enterprise relating to money.

Fixed costs: Costs that stay the same despite changes in the activity of the enterprise.

Formal: Conventional, polite, respectful and official.

Founders: The people who start a company.

Franchise: A form of business organisation that allows a company (franchisee) to buy the right to use an existing company's (franchisor) brand name and products/service.

Goods: The finished product sold by an enterprise to its customers.

Gross profit: Revenue minus cost of sales.

Identify: Name/select/recognise.

Import duties: A tax to be paid by a business to the government for importing goods from another country.

Income: All the money that comes in to an enterprise.

Informal: Relaxed, friendly and unofficial.

Interest: Often, when an enterprise borrows money from a lender they will have to pay back the amount they borrow plus an agreed amount. The additional amount is known as the interest.

Internal sources of finance: Money that is found within the enterprise.

Jargon: Special words or phrases that are used by a particular group or industry that are not commonly used by everybody.

Justify: Support a case with evidence/argument.

Knowledge: The theoretical facts and information that you gather through your experience or education.

Limited company: An incorporated business that is a separate legal entity from its owners.

Limited liability: Shareholders/owners are only liable to pay or lose the amount they have invested.

Loss: When the total income of the enterprise is less than the total expenditure of the enterprise.

Market research: The process of collecting, collating and analysing data about customers, competitors or a market.

Marketing: Anticipating, identifying and satisfying customer needs.

Materials: The raw components (such as ingredients for a cake) that are needed to make the finished goods.

Mentor: An expert/experienced person who agrees to provide dedicated advice and support.

Micro loans: Small amounts of money that can be borrowed more easily than by a traditional bank loan.

Minutes: A document giving a clear and accurate record of the meeting.

Monitor: To check or review the progress of something over a period of time.

Negotiation: The process of discussion in order to reach agreement on a course of action (or solve a dispute) that satisfies the interests of all involved.

Net profit: Gross profit minus all other expenditures of the enterprise (often called overheads) that are not directly linked to generating sales.

Glossary

Objective: A specific target that an enterprise wants to reach so it can achieve its aims.

Opportunity: A time or event that makes it possible to do something.

Overheads: Net profit minus all other expenditure.

Partnership: A business that is owned by two or more people, known as the partners. This sort of a business organisation is unincorporated and so the partners have unlimited liability.

Prepare: Present information in a suitable format.

Primary research (field research): Collecting new information or data for a specific purpose.

Profit: When the total income of the enterprise is greater than the total expenditure of the enterprise.

Receiver: An organisation/group/individual to whom a message is sent.

Revenue: The money that comes into an enterprise from selling goods and services. To work out revenue you do a simple calculation: selling price x quantity sold = revenue.

Reward: Something given in recognition of effort or return for something achieved.

Risk: The chance of gaining or losing something as a result of an action taken.

Secondary research (desk research): The use of information that already exists and was originally collected for a different purpose.

Seed capital: The money needed to start a business. This money often comes from the owner's personal assets and their friends and family.

Sender: An organisation/group/individual attempting to get their message to others.

Service: Something that an enterprise might do for their customers (such as cleaning their windows).

Skills: Your ability to do something. This can be something that you were born with such as a natural ability to encourage and motivate people, or it could be something that you have learnt such as time management.

Slang: Words or phrases that might be used when chatting with family or friends informally.

Social Enterprise: An organisation that is started up for social cause for the betterment of society.

Sole trader: A business that is owned and run by just one person though it may employ staff. It is an unincorporated business in which the owner has unlimited liability for all the debts of the business.

Source of finance: The way in which an enterprise gets the money it needs to finance an activity.

Sponsorship: An enterprise paying or offering something in return for having its name linked with an event, person or group.

Stakeholder: An individual, group or organisation with an interest in the activities of a business.

Start-up: The period of an enterprise when it is first set up.

State: Express in clear terms.

Supplier: A person or organisation that provides the goods/materials or services that an enterprise needs in order to operate.

Surplus: On a cash flow forecast, if the cash that comes into the enterprise is greater than the cash that goes out, there is a surplus of cash.

Tariff: A tax/charge to be paid by a business to the government for importing (buying goods from other countries) and exporting (selling goods to other countries).

Total costs: The total of the variable costs + fixed costs.

Trade barriers: Steps taken by the government to control international trade. An example would be charging a tax on imports.

Trade payable: The amount of money owed by the enterprise to suppliers, such as for raw material received but not paid for.

Trade receivable: The amount of money owed to the enterprise by customers who have had goods or services but not yet paid for them.

Unincorporated business: A business that does not possess a separate legal identity from its owner. The owner(s) have full liability for the business.

Unlimited liability: Shareholders/owners are liable for all the debts of their organisation and stand to lose their investment as well as personal assets if the business goes into debt.

Variable costs: Costs that increase and decrease with the activity of the enterprise.

Note: Page numbers followed by f or t represent figures or tables respectively.

A

action plan
    checklist, 76–77
    defined, 65
    format of, 66f
    importance of, 66
    monitoring, methods of, 69–70, 69f
    purpose of, 66
    stages of, 67f
    updating, importance of, 70
advertising, 109
agenda, meeting, 136–137, 137f
aims
    activities of enterprises and, 65
    defined, 64
    marketing and, 104–105
    objectives *vs.*, 64
analysis, 8, 160
    developing depth to, 163–164
    skills, 161–162
apologies, 136
asset loans, 152
assets, 83
audience, 131

B

bank/building society loan, 80t
bank overdrafts, 80t
bar charts, 56, 56f
Beauchamp, Josh, 82
Blathwayt, Flora, 82
BLT ('because,' 'leads to' and 'therefore'), 164
break-even point, 93, 97–98, 97f, 98t, 173
Budd, Tanya, 30–31
business enterprise, 3. *see also* enterprise
business licensing, 150
business networks, 153
business organisations, types of, 15–20, 15f
    co-operatives, 19
    franchises, 19
    limited companies, 17–18
    partnerships, 16–17
    social enterprises, 19–20
    sole trader, 16

business plans
    contents of, 71
    defined, 70
    importance of, 71
    monitoring methods, 73
    purpose of, 71
    for Suki's Noodle Bar, 72–73
    updating, reasons for, 73–74, 74f

C

cash flow, 90
    forecast, 94–96, 172
cash inflow, 94
cash outflow, 94
charities, 20, 152
communication
    formal, 133t
    informal, 131, 134
    internal, 178–179
    marketing, 109–112, 110–111t, 176–177
    non-verbal, 132, 133t
    types of, 131
    verbal, 132
community sources, as external source of finance, 81t
competition, 6
consumer panels, 51
consumers, 6
co-operatives
    advantages of, 19
    defined, 19
    disadvantages of, 19
costs, 98. *see also* specific types
crowdfunding, as external source of finance, 82t
customer retention
    defined, 105
    measurement methods, 106–107
    methods, 107–108
    strategies, 108
customers, 6
    defined, 90
    trade credit between enterprises and, 90
customer satisfaction
    defined, 106
    measurement methods, 106–107

D

decision-making, 4
deficit, 94
describe, 23
desk market research. *see* secondary/desk market research
discuss, 23

E

employees, 5
employment contracts, 43
enterprise process, 12–14, 12f
    action planning, 13
    creative solutions, 13
    defined, 12
    monitoring progress, 13–14
    plan implementation, 13
    problem identification, 12–13
enterprises
    action plan. *see* action plan
    activities, aims and, 65
    aims. *see* aims
    business plans. *see* business plans
    capability, attributes comprising, 4
    characteristics of, 3
    and customer retention. *see* customer retention
    defined, 3
    help and support for. *see* help and support
    marketing. *see* marketing
    opportunities, 34
    process of. *see* enterprise process
    purpose of, 3
    risks. *see* risks
    social, 3
    stakeholders in, 5–6, 5f
    start-up, 79, 79t–82t
    trade credit. *see* trade credit
enterprising people
    behaviours of, 30–31
    skills of, 26, 26f
entrepreneurs, 4
    help and support for, 155–156
ethics, 44–45
evaluation, 8, 160, 165–168
    skills, 161–162

evidence, 164
expenditure, 99
    projected, 102
explain, 8
external sources of finance, 80t–82t, 83

F

Fajarai, Benny, 34
field market research. *see* primary/field market research
finance
    defined, 79
    sources of. *see* sources of finance
fixed costs, 98t
focus groups, 51, 107
formal communication, non-verbal communication and, 133t
formal reports, 143–144
formal sources, of help and support
    business networks, 153
    consultants, 151
    financial institutions, 151–152
    government/business agencies, 149–150
    teachers, 152
formal written communications, 131
founders, 83
franchise
    advantages of, 19
    defined, 19
    disadvantages of, 19
friends and family members, as help and support source, 154

G

Girl Child Network Worldwide, 21
goods, 90
government, as stakeholder, 6
government/business agencies, 149–150
grants, 81t
graphs, 57, 57f
gross profit, 99

H

Happy Feet, 9
help and support
    for entrepreneurs, 155–156
    formal sources. *see* formal sources, of help and support

Index

informal sources, 154
sources of, 149
suitability of sources, 154
home, ways of enterprising at, 7f
Hypo-Hoist, 30

I
identify, 8
import duties, 150
income, 20
    projected, 102
income statement, 93, 99–100, 173
informal communication, 131, 134
informal sources, of help and support, 154
innovation, 4
interest, 79
internal communication, 178–179
internal sources of finance, 79, 79t
interviews, 51

J
jargon, 131
justify, 109

K
knowledge, enterprising people, 26
Kroc, Ray, 22
Kumar, Arjun Santoth, 27–28

L
leasing, as external source of finance, 80t
legal obligations, 43–44
lenders, 6
limited company
    advantages of, 17–18
    defined, 17
    disadvantages of, 18
    private, 17
    public, 17
    types of, 17
limited liability, 17
listening skills, for negotiation, 123–124
loans
    asset, 152
    bank/building society, 80t
    micro, 151–152
local community, as stakeholder, 6

lose-lose outcome, negotiation, 119
loss, 97

M
Makoni, Betty, 21
marketing
    communication, 109–112, 110–111t, 176–177
    customer retention. *see* customer retention
    defined, 104
    and enterprise aims, 104–105
    method, selection of, 113–114
market research, 170–171
    conducting, 60–61
    data, 58
    defined, 50
    primary, 50–51
    purpose of, 50
    secondary, 53–54
materials, 91
McDonald, Maurice, 22
McDonald, Richard, 22
McDonald's, 22–23
meetings, 134, 179–180
    agenda, 136–137, 137f
    attending, 139
    evaluating, 139–140, 140t
    key roles in, 137–138
    minutes of, 138f
    organising, 135–137
    planning and holding effective, 146–147
    reasons for, 134–135
mentors, 153
micro loans, 151–152
Mintz, Noa, 34
minutes, 136
monitoring
    action plans, 69–70, 69f
    business plans, 73
    defined, 69
    in enterprise process, 13–14
    risks, 42
mortgages, as external source of finance, 81t
Mupuya, Andrew, 40, 43

N

negotiation
- conducting, 126–127
- defined, 118
- planning. *see* planning, negotiation
- process of, 118
- purpose of, 118
- role of, 118
- skills required for, 123–124
- success measurement, 127–128
- win-win outcome, 119

net profit, 100
Network for Teaching Entrepreneurship (NFTE), 152
non-verbal communication, 132, 133t
not-for-profit enterprises, 19–20
not-for-profit organisations, 152

O

objectives, 64–65
- aims *vs.*, 64
- defined, 64

observations, 51
opportunities, enterprise, 34
overheads, 100
owners/shareholders, 5

P

partnerships
- advantages, 17
- defined, 16
- disadvantages, 17

personal savings, as sources of finance, 79t
persuasion, as negotiation, 123
PEST analysis, 38, 38t
- conducting, 47

pie charts, 56, 56f
planning, 169
planning, negotiation, 118
- objectives, setting, 118–119
- proposal, arguments and counter arguments for, 121
- proposal, benefits and weaknesses of, 121
- success measurement, 127–128
- template of, 122

positive attitude, 4
prepare, defined, 66
presentations, 134–135, 141–143
- handouts in, guidance for using, 142
- slides in, guidance for using, 142
- visual aids in, guidance for using, 143

primary/field market research
- defined, 50
- effectiveness of, 54, 54t
- examples of, 50–51
- results presentation, 55–57

private limited company, 17
profits, 94
- gross, 99
- net, 100

proposal
- arguments and counter arguments for, 121
- benefits and weaknesses of, 121
- presenting, 125

public limited company, 17

Q

quantitative data, 50
questionnaires, 50–51, 106

R

raw materials, 91
receiver, 131
reports, 134–135
- formal, 143–144
- sections of, 143–144

revenue, 89
rewards, 34
risk-averse attitude, 42
risk-keen attitude, 42
risk management, 36
- stages of, 37–42, 37f
- strategies, 41

risk-reducer attitude, 42
risks, 35f
- attitudes to, 42
- consequences, 40
- defined, 35
- identification of, 37–40
- managing. *see* risk management
- monitoring, 42
- reducing, 42

risk-taking, 4, 36

Index

S
Samphire Festival, UK, 82
school, ways of enterprising at, 7f
secondary/desk market research
    defined, 53
    effectiveness of, 54, 54t
    examples of, 53
    results presentation, 55–57
seed capital, 152
sender, 131
service, 90
SEZ. *see* special economic zones (SEZ)
shareholders, 5
shares, as external source of finance, 82t
skills, enterprising people, 26, 26f
    evaluation of, 28
    identification of, 28
skills, for negotiation
    listening, 123–124
    persuasion, 123
skills audit, 29
slang, 131
SMART (specific, measurable, achievable, realistic and time-based) objectives, 64
social enterprises, 3
    advantages of, 20
    charities, 20
    defined, 19
    disadvantages of, 20
    not-for-profit enterprises, 19–20
sole trader
    advantages, 16
    defined, 16
    disadvantages, 16
Someshwar, Nirali, 9
sources of finance, 171–172
    choosing, 87
    for continuing trading and expansion, 83, 83t–85t
    defined, 79
    external, 80t–82t, 83
    internal, 79
    for start-up enterprises, 79t–81t
special economic zones (SEZ), 150
sponsorship, 111

stakeholders
    defined, 4
    in enterprise, 5–6, 5f
start-up enterprises, 90, 97
    defined, 79
    sources of finance for, 79t–81t
state, 23
subsidies, 81t, 149
Subway, 19
suppliers, 6
    defined, 89
    trade credit between enterprises and, 89–90
surplus, 94
surveys, 50–51, 106
SWOT analysis, 38–40, 38t
    conducting, 48

T
tables, 56, 56f
tariff, 150
tax incentives, 149
test marketing, 51
total costs, 98t
trade barriers, 150
trade credit
    between enterprises and customers, 90
    between enterprises and suppliers, 89–90
trade payables, 89–90
trade receivables, 90

U
Umm Al Moumineen Women's Association, 150–151
unincorporated business, 16
unlimited liability, 16

V
variable costs, 98t
verbal communications, 132

W
win-lose/lose-win outcome, negotiation, 119
win-win outcome, negotiation, 119
written communications, 131

The authors and publishers acknowledge the following sources of copyright material and are grateful for the permissions granted. While every effort has been made, it has not always been possible to identify the sources of all the material used, or to trace all copyright holders. If any omissions are brought to our notice, we will be happy to include the appropriate acknowledgements on reprinting.

Thanks to the following for permission to reproduce images:

Cover image: Ashley Cooper/Getty Images

Chapter Opener 0 Andrew Baker/Ikon Images/Getty Images; Chapter Opener 1 Yagi StudioGetty Images; Fig 1.3b CommerceandCultureAgency/Getty Images; Fig 1.4 Tim Boyle/Getty Images; Chapter Opener 2 Morsa Images/Getty Images; Fig 2.3 Dinodia Photo/Passage/Getty Images; Fig 2.5 Seasafe Sytems; Chapter Opener 3 belterz/Getty Images; Fig 3.4 Matthias Kulka/Corbis/Getty Images; Chapter Opener 4 Stuart Kinlough/Ikon Images/Getty Images; Fig 4.1 Yuri_Arcurs/DigitalVision/Getty Images; Fig 4.2 Gam1983/iStock/Getty Images Plus; Fig 4.3 Chee Siong Teh/EyeEm/Getty Images; Chapter Opener 5 KatarzynaBialasiewicz/iStock/Getty Images Plus; Fig 5.3 Moriyu/Moment/Getty Images; Chapter Opener 6 Adrienne Bresnahan/Moment/Getty Images; Fig 6.1 Samphire Festival; Chapter Opener 7 Bob O'Connor/The Image Bank/Getty Images; Chapter Opener 8 Urbancow/Getty Images; Fig 8.1 Blueringmedia/iStock/Getty Images Plus; Chapter Opener 9 WIN-Initiative/Getty Images; Fig 9.1 Rawpixel/iStock/Getty Images Plus; Fig 9.2 Glegorly/iStock/Getty Images Plus; Fig 9.3 Geography Photos/Universal Images Group/Getty Images; Fig 9.4 PressureUA/iStock Editorial/Getty Images Plus; Fig 9.5 Thinglass/iStock Editorial/Getty Images Plus; Chapter Opener 10 Instants/E+/Getty Images; Fig 10.1 Alistaircotton/iStock/Getty Images Plus; Fig 10.3 Peshkova/iStock/Getty Images Plus; Fig 10.4 Suriyapong/iStock/Getty Images Plus; Chapter Opener 11 Andrew Brookes/Cultura/Getty Images; Aleutie/Shutterstock; Fig 11.7 Morsa Images/Taxi/Getty Images; Chapter Opener 12 Sally ElfordGetty Images; Fig 12.1 JohnnyGreig/E+/Getty Images; Fig 12.2 Holgs/E+/Getty Images; Fig 12.3 Inti St Clair/Blend Images/Getty Images; Chapter Opener 13 Image Source/Getty Images; Fig 13.1 Heliography/Stockimo/Alamy Stock Photo;